A Is for Animals is a wo
the rich and deep emotion
animals, including cats, dogs, fishes, and parrots. It is an 'easy read' and a 'fun' book for people of all ages. In an increasingly human-dominated world, nonhumans need all the help they can get, and Svetlana Alexander's book is just what is needed to get people to treat other animals with respect, dignity, and love.

—Marc Bekoff, author of *The Animals' Agenda: Freedom, Compassion, and Coexistence in the Human Age* (with Jessica Pierce) and *Canine Confidential: Why Dogs Do What They Do.*

A IS FOR ANIMALS

True Stories about the
Emotional Lives of Animals

SVETLANA ALEXANDER

ISBN: Softcover 978-0-692-05350-8

Photo credits

Egyptian goose © Alta Oosthuizen / 123rf.com
Back cover image ©ThanapolKuptanisacorn / 123rf.com
Collie ©moaphotography / 123rf.com

This book was printed in the United States of America

First paperback edition published by CreateSpace in 2018

https://www.facebook.com/svetinol

This Book is for my Children and Grandchildren:
Elena and Pavel, Daniel, Alex, Nastya, and Roman

CONTENTS

Introduction

One can accuse me of anything—being naïve, romantic, anthropomorphic but not unscientific. Holding the highest scientific degree in Solid State Physics, I accidentally touched base with a softer matter, animals' relations, and made curious observations on this subject. Because I never had prejudices against animals and considered myself merely as a part of their vast world, I attributed reasoning and emotions to dogs, cats, birds, and even fish. Wonder and amazement were my first reactions that fueled my curiosity, pushing my mind to make associations with known human behavior. In my collection of short stories, I don't chase new theories, nor do I try to classify animal behavior I happened to observe; rather I simply describe animals in their relationships with each other and with people. My stories are unique, as unique as the individual personalities of animals.

The title *Three Cats in One House* speaks for itself. Once upon a time, three cats used to live in our house. Beloved Matisse, an explorer, admired Cezanne, a hunter, and a stray Maine Coon feline who fell in love with my husband and took command over the house as soon as she was allowed to stay.

The story *The Way Our Animals Love Us* is about my daughter Lena's family pets in Siberia and their unconditional love for humans. The cat, Monya, adopted Lena's baby, serving as a playmate and nanny. A Cocker Spaniel provided comfort and companionship to Lena's husband as he was dying from cancer, and Mensch, the neighbor's guard dog, who never knew human tenderness until he abandoned his duties and moved to Lena's house, finding love and final resort there.

Impressions is a small collection of my minute observations of bird life in the Arenberg Castle Park in Belgium. The objects of my "research" were a tyrant swan terrorizing the entire community, an outcast family of Egyptian geese, and the sexual adventures of ducks.

Birds Differ in Their Mind is a story about Prosha the Parakeet, an amazing little bird with a great mind. This minuscule brain-machine, Savant, not only mastered nine hundred words but also developed a taste for poetry.

Unlike many Americans, I never intended to write anything but my scientific papers, and in my wildest dreams I wouldn't imagine myself writing about fish. However, a scene I observed in Tsukuba, Japan in 2006 instantly materialized into the story *Japanese Delights*. Some time later a scientific paper by James Rose and his six colleagues was published, in which the authors concluded that fish can't see, can't hear, and can't feel, all in strict contradiction to my observation and reasoning. However, the results of the studies discussed in Jonathan Balcombe's superb book *What a Fish Knows*, published recently, proved the authors of that notorious paper wrong. "Fishes are individuals with minds and memories, able to plan, capable of recognizing others, equipped with instincts and able to learn from experience," concluded Balcombe.

Open Letter from a Dog is a satire directed against those who still doubt animals' intellect and their rich emotional life.

Birds Differ in Their Mind

The Zoology Museum was as old as Tomsk State University itself, Siberia's first university, founded in 1887. The museum housed over a hundred thousand exhibits, including a collection of seventeen thousand birds. Entering a few minutes earlier than my appointment, I found myself in a huge hall packed with stuffed animals, birds, insects, and reptiles preserved in formalin.

In a corner not far from the entrance, a gigantic bird cage with numerous perches sat atop a large table. In it, I discovered two tiny parrots. A tablet on the cage provided their Latin name *Melopsittackus Undulatus*, with "Wavy parrots" in parentheses. In a minute, a bell rang, announcing a break between classes. Soon after, Andrei Petrovich emerged from an adjacent classroom. In his forties, his manners soft, his voice pleasant, he matched the mental portrait I drew during our phone conversation.

"Here you are! Glad to see you, Irina," he said, shaking my hand.

"Hello, Andrei Petrovich. Sorry for intruding. The door was unlocked."

"No problem." He motioned to the cage. "Here are the guys I was talking about. Two months old, fully-fledged, and weaned. Best time for adoption."

"They're gorgeous but so tiny! You said 'weaned.' Does that mean the chick can feed itself?"

"Well, it will, but you should teach it anyway." Looking at me intently, he added, "You're the mother, and that is what's expected of the mother. Right?"

"Sure."

"Now, about the cage. You will need one with a twenty-inch perimeter, and keep it out of direct sunlight!" He stared at me. "Remember, Irina, you have to teach the chick everything the way you would teach a child."

"Yes, I know. I've read about this on the internet."

"Good. Don't handle the chick during the first few days at home, leave it in the cage. Just approach and coo. When you speak, put yourself at the bird's level, not higher.

"What else?"

"Well, when the chick gets accustomed to you, don't keep it imprisoned."

I nodded. "When should we expect it to start talking?"

"Depends on you, Irina. Normally, at five or six months. But it will entertain you anyway unless cats are around. No cats!"

He waved his index finger at me, crinkled his nose, and partly opened his mouth, lifting his upper lip as if a dog showing its teeth in a snarl. "No cats! Either cat or parrot. Keep this in mind. Now, let's choose. Here we have two chicks—both boys, almost identical, except for the color. If you're looking for a talker, that is what you need—a male and single one. Otherwise, he'll spend all his brain thinking about a girlfriend."

Fascinated, I was staring at the birds, both adorable—one a bright-yellowish-green, the other a delicate snow-white. I reached out to the cage and touched its wires. The green bird immediately retreated to the back of the cage and bristled up, trembling. But the white chick, separated from his sibling, approached the partition between the wires. Stretching his neck, he explored my index finger with his beak. Thus it happened. The little fellow chose me himself.

Andrei Petrovich opened the cage, caught the bird, and placed it into the kefir box I brought with me.

"Good luck!" He gave his blessing. "Hurry, Irina, to reduce his stress. And don't hesitate to call me." He handed me a page filled with neat handwriting. "Here is a list of instructions."

"Thank you very much, I appreciate you selecting me as parent. I'll do my best. *Dosvidanjya.*"

This is the way our journey started. The chick was cute and touchingly helpless. During his first days he shied away from me and my husband, Sergey, so we advanced slowly. First, we needed a name. Since we wanted to treat the birdlike a human baby, we christened him Prosha. Why Prosha? To distinguish him from others parrots in Russia, all called Kesha—the name of a parrot character in a popular cartoon. To encourage Prosha's sense of freedom, we even avoided using words related to captivity. The cage, we called an "aviary" or "birdhouse," or just a "little house" (*domik*). Sergey made two perches, one inside the *domik* and another, about three feet long, from the *domik's* door to the window.

It took Prosha a while to learn perching. At first, he could barely keep a balance at a six-foot height. Later, I taught him how to walk along the outside perch and to enter the *domik*. First, he stepped on my finger, then into or out of the birdhouse. Thank God, he did not need to use a key. I fed him by hand until he learned to nibble from a bird feeder.

And of course, I talked to our baby boy every day, never missing a chance to caress him. Once Prosha was settled in his new quarters, we started introducing toys. At first he was suspicious but became accustomed fast, closely examining the toys, playing with a tennis ball and with cubes half the size of his body. Mastering football, he pushed the ball with his foot or beak. Occasionally, the football rebounded from an obstacle and collided with Prosha, turning him over on his back—always a surprise. Like all parrots, he liked swinging.

Prosha's favorite toy was a small bell hanging on the perch in the *domik*. He would tap the bell repeatedly and listen to the sound. To avoid accidents, we locked Prosha in the *domik* each night and also when we went out; however, we never covered the cage with a cloth. Soon Prosha learned to retire himself after a request was issued, "Enough, enough, Prosha. Go to the *domik*! Sleep!" But occasionally, Prosha showed his character by disobeying.

Usually, it happened when we came home late and had no time to chat with him. If we retired, ignoring Prosha's playful mood, he would enter the *domik* murmuring and turn his bristled up back to us, demonstrating his disappointment. Mornings, he always woke early and waited silently for us, never disturbing our sleep. As soon as he noticed one of us had open eyes, he would start pecking at his bell, and there was no staying in bed longer.

Once, about two months after Prosha's adoption, I entered the apartment holding grocery bags in both hands and proceeded straight to the kitchen without acknowledging his presence. Bustling around, stowing groceries, I paid no attention to his persistent chirping in the *domik*. Suddenly, my ears caught the repeated patterns: "Unlock Prosha! Unlock Prosha!" I froze in amazement.

Yes, "Unlock Prosha!" I abandoned the kitchen and rushed to my boy.

"Prosha, good boy! I love you. Let's kiss." I kept repeating, taking him into my hands.

"Unlock Prosha," was his first phrase. Gradually, his vocabulary expanded, and in six months he could comment on events and say short verses he had learned. Perching next to the window, Prosha updated us on the outdoor conditions like a weatherman: "It is raining . . . Snowing . . . Snow flakes flitting . . . Sunshine . . . Is summer soon?" Indeed, most of all, he liked summer.

Prosha's communication skills developed quickly. A couple of toy parrots nailed to the perch were his buddies. At first, he tried to feed them from his beak, keeping saying to them: "Come on, take it! Don't bite! Don't bite!" Having failed with nursing, he would start chirping: "You are a parrot with such small claws."

While coaching them in the art of flying, Prosha would raise his wings and tiptoe. He demonstrated to them how to take off from the perch, remaining in the cage, or taking off and flying out of the cage. Those dumb fellows never followed his ingenious instructions. Disappointed Prosha would jerk and stand back, cocking his head and staring at his pupils. Exasperated, he might peck at them and yell: "Come on! What is it with you?" Observing how those hopeless training sessions exhausted Prosha, we decided to ease his burden and removed one of the obstinate creatures from the cage. At last, he lost interest in one-way communication.

Prosha was affectionate towards both Sergey and me, always calling us by name, but invariably, he showed a deeper intimacy with me. When I came home after long office hours, a few cheerful Prosha's greetings would wipe away all my stress: "Irochka, Mommy, she worked, I missed her, I was alone, I am hurt, let's kiss." Then he would land on my shoulder and step onto my chin or nose, and kiss, uttering: "I love you so much." Riding on my head, while I walked around the apartment, was a special act of recognition that none of our relatives or friends received.

Prosha's relationship with Sergey was more complicated. Though he had great affection for my husband, Prosha could also be rough, demanding, and bossy. After his work, Sergey usually hibernated on a couch in the living area while I, locked off in the kitchen, was busy preparing dinner. Abandoned by the family, Prosha would become upset and withdraw into his *domik*. Once safely there, he would start scolding Sergey: "Why don't you talk to me? Why are you lying there?"

Annoyed by Prosha's preaching, Sergey would throw back something impersonal. But Prosha, feeling his detachment, chided: "Lying Sergey still loves Prosha." If that trick did not work, Prosha would get angry and yell: "Come on. Why are you lying there? Bring me the biscuit!"

There was no way to ignore him longer, and Sergey obediently delivered the requested snack. When I would eventually emerge from the kitchen, Prosha flew to my shoulder and tried to penetrate my mouth with his beak to provide me service as fish cleaners do, feeding on those delicacies stuck between the teeth of their clients.

Once, Sergey was away on a trip for ten days. When he finally returned, Prosha was perching next to the window. As soon as Sergey stepped in into the apartment, Prosha hurled his body in the air and in the blink of an eye roosted on Sergey's head. Out of my husband's sight, he confessed shyly: "*Papochka*, love you!" Then he climbed down to Sergey's shoulder closer to his chest to take care of Sergey's mustache. Pulling each hair, one by one, through his beak, he performed a ritual female birds provide to their beloved ones.

Occasionally, Sergey drank too much, and, of course, I scolded him. Sergey never argued. He just leaned closer to the TV set, and the dispute was over. Once, I persisted: "Look, you better stop before you become an alcoholic!" This was the only time I used the word "alcoholic" in Prosha's presence. Several months later, Sergey came home drunk again. I did not wish to start a quarrel and withdrew into my kitchen fortress, leaving the door open. Preening in the *domik*, Prosha also boycotted Sergey, and grave silence pervaded. Suddenly I heard Prosha take flight. I poked my head out the door and noticed him passing Sergey. "Alcoholic! Alcoholic!" he yelled. Joining me in the kitchen, he landed onto my shoulder. I locked the door, and we caressed each other.

Prosha didn't welcome all visitors equally. Certain new-comers, he pushed away as soon as they would step in: "Why you came? Go home!" With chosen ones, he engaged in long conversations.

"*Privet*!"

"*Privet*!"

"What you brought?" He usually asked.

"Something for you."

"What? Tell me."

"An apple."

"Where is it?" After our visitor provided an apple, Prosha would continue, "How is it outside?"

"Well, kinda warm."

"Summer soon," Prosha would conclude.

On one occasion a visitor admitted, "I'm kinda tired, I need more sleep." To this, Prosha immediately exploded. "Go home to sleep!"

Once my aunt Rita decided to stay for the night at our place, and I made her bed on the couch, across from Prosha's *domik*.

Immediately Prosha got mad, "No, go home! Go home!"

Aunt Rita was speechless. It was a late hour, and her train had already departed. When the light was off, Prosha continued muttering discontented, sulkily settling into his *domik* for the night.

In general, Prosha had no interest in the TV, and I guessed he simply disliked its competition for our attention. On one occasion, I borrowed a camcorder to make a movie of him. While I was reviewing the recording on the TV screen, Prosha was preening. Then suddenly he admitted, "Mommy, I love you."

I merely nodded in response, watching his movie. But this was not what he expected. So, he appealed for my attention again, "Prosha little chick, Prosha good boy."

Having exhausted his flamboyant repertoire, my cavalier finally took off and rested on my head. In the wall mirror, I saw him following his own actions on the TV for a few minutes. Perhaps disappointed with what he saw, he took off and headed to the *domik*, yelling, "Cheater! Cheater! Cheater!" accusing the bird on the screen for stealing my affection.

With the phone he always enjoyed participating in conversations.

"*Privet*!" He always echoed to a caller.

"Who is this?" was a usual reply.

"Prosha Berdyshev."

"Prosha, *Privet*. Where do you live?"

"Prosha Berdyshev lives in Tomsk." And so on with variations. At the end of the call he would invariably invite: "Come, visit us!"

While talking to Andrei Petrovich, the ornithologist, Prosha asked him, "Who are you?" After Andrei Petrovich had identified himself, Prosha invited him over. Andrei Petrovich cracked up, laughing. "Never could imagine a parrot would invite me for a visit! You're a character, Prosha!"

Indeed, our parrot became such a celebrity that we had visitors all the time. Once, my aunt Sandra from the United States, appeared. The rumors about our bird had reached her on the opposite side of the globe. On that occasion, Prosha seemed reserved. He even refused to step out of his *domik* unless there was a chance to sit on me, on my face in particular. Planting one of his feet onto my chin and another above the upper lip, he kissed me and shyly hid under my chin. For some reason, he was not in a talking mood. Instead of coaxing him, we retreated to the kitchen. From time to time Prosha dispatched brief messages to which we paid no attention.

All of a sudden my aunt pressed a finger to her lips, pointing at the door. "Shh! Do you hear? What's this?"

"Prosha is talking."

She listened intently. "Kind of a rhyme, but too quick for me to catch up."

"His forte, *Fly Zokotuha* by Korney Chukovsky," I prompted.

She was enthralled.

I gestured, inviting her to the performance. "Yes, he likes tales and verses."

"Look, this isn't a short piece. A good hundred lines, one of my favorites. My grandson, four, doesn't recite it by heart," she whispered.

We tiptoed into the living room and sat on the couch. Perching in his quarters, as if on a stage, Prosha was in a trance. My aunt, a physicist, was stunned. It seemed Prosha's acting triggered her research instinct.

"Irina, how did you teach him?"

"I didn't. How could I with no time on my hands?"

"But how did he learn all this?"

"Well, there are two of us, Sergey and myself. While we talk to each other, Prosha is always around. And, of course, I talk to Prosha."

"But I read that one must repeat again and again the same word for a parrot to memorize. And you say he has figured all this out himself?"

"Yes, Prosha learned all this as a child would."

"Well, to learn from interaction, he had to connect sounds with the object or its image. To do so, he needs experience. I read a book by Lorenz, a naturalist. "Parrots just imitate words,' he said."

"I know that book. It's a hundred years old!" I noted.

"And what? In a hundred years parrots developed human brains?"

"Andrei Petrovich told us Grey parrots learn speech from social interaction."

My aunt got excited. "But this is not a Grey parrot! It's a Wavy parrot, budgie perhaps. What brain size can Prosha have? Look at it! What else did this ornithologist tell you?"

"Andrey Petrovich used to come to record Prosha's speech. It turned out he himself hadn't seen anything like Prosha before. He told us Prosha is a member of our family or flock, and the flock may share a common mental or intellectual culture. Like Prosha's brain is tuned to ours."

But my aunt insisted, "Well, Prosha has a bird's brain, and that is a fact. What is his vocabulary?"

I started losing my patience. "Don't you hear yourself? The piece he just recited might have a hundred words!"

"Never mind. He's just mimicking," she pressed firmly.

"Mimicking?" I got furious. "We used to write down all his words but stopped when the list reached nine hundred."

"Well, I read that parrots can memorize a hundred words, but nine hundred . . . " She stared at Prosha. Prosha stared at her.

Leaning back on the couch, I decided to relax. Her critique was nothing new for me. "Can't help you! Nine hundred. His very first words were 'Unlock Prosha!' He caught the phrase and made the right connection."

There was a silence between us for a moment. "Then other words came, like 'Prosha chick, little one, Prosha good boy, let's kiss, I missed you.'"

"Sure. You used those words while petting, and he mimicked them successfully," she insisted.

I brought another argument. "But poems and fairy tales! Have you ever heard parakeets reciting?"

"These are all abstractions for a bird. Prosha can't make any associations without experience. A bird's brain is innocent of all those characters in the books. Completely."

"Well, I do not know about that. I just was reading to him and noticed he liked it."

Although I was tired of being defensive, she continued her interrogation. "And then?"

"Then he would settle on my chest and ask, 'Mommy, read me a fairytale.' I would ask which one, and he would reply, '*Fly Zokotuha* or *A Bear.*' So I did. If I had delayed, he would get impatient, repeating his request."

While we squabbled, Prosha took a break, preening his pretty, silver plumage. He seemed to be ignoring us, showing off like a kid in the presence of strangers.

"So what does Prosha Berdyshev like?" My aunt asked.

"He likes Korney Chukovsky and Agnia Barto. Especially, Barto's poems *Chicken and an Egg, Bear Bandy-Legged, A Little Bull.* He used to settle on my chest and listen intently, looking into my mouth, never interrupting me."

My aunt turned to the artist, "Prosha, tell us *Bear Bandy-Legged.*"

Prosha gazed at us intently, swaying his head. I repeated, "Prosha, tell us *Bear Bandy-Legged.*" No response.

She glanced at the clock on the wall, picked up her purse and tossed her slippers into the corner. "I must hurry to meet my friend," she said, rising from the couch.

At this moment, Prosha started his quick chatter, reciting *Bear Bandy-Legged.*

My aunt dropped back onto the couch, staring at Prosha. Moved by his reciting, she applauded. "Fantastic! So, Irina, he started repeating after you those fairy tales and verses." This time she made a statement instead of an argument.

"Look at him! He's getting impatient because we're talking while he recites." The artist needs our full attention, so I encouraged him, "Prosha is a good boy."

Now perching in his *domik*, he was reciting self-forgetfully:

"Prosha is a bird parakeet.
Birds differ in their mind
And in their quick wits.
There are birds
That chirp and sing,
They fly
And live in delight."

"What? What did he say, birds differ in what?" She asked.

"'Birds differ in their mind and their quick wits,'" I repeated. "This is a piece from that animation about the parakeet Kesha."

"Wow! Prosha, now you got me." She surrendered, savoring the performance in a total oblivion. After a pause, she noted, "Prosha was moody in the beginning, and now he's in complete control."

"Well, he can be as emotional as me. You know I am hyper, and recently found out why, because of my thyroid. But Prosha can be affectionate, dissatisfied, stubborn, cunning, scared, jealous, and unhappy. By now I know all his facial expressions."

My aunt laughed. Having approached Prosha's *domik*, she looked at him fixedly. "I don't see any facial expressions."

"It comes with time. Prosha's eyes, his voice, a particular look, and certain actions. For instance, his face gets elongated when he is surprised and shrinks when he gets scared."

My aunt was intrigued. Leaving, she promised to do research on Wavy parrots back in the US. I was curious to know what she would come up with.

One year later, I developed symptoms of acute hyperthyroidism. At the same time, Prosha's health worsened. He was losing his feathers. His claws and beak started growing excessively, to the degree that he experienced difficulties perching and eating, and his thyroid became very hard to the touch—a sorry sight. It was clear that Prosha's metabolism was severely affected. We couldn't really do much, though everybody tried to help. Each new day, the tiny fire of Prosha's life faded. First, he became unable to feed himself. Then he could not hold the perch anymore. Prosha slept with me on the pillow, and one morning I found him dead.

Andrey Petrovich believed Prosha's thyroid problem was related to my own. Being empathic, parrots may develop diseases and symptoms similar to those they love. Sergey and I could not easily accept Prosha's death, and his many fans joined us in grieving. Why did such a lovely and happy being leave us so prematurely? Others wondered whose soul had lived in the bird, for they could not accept that Prosha might have had a soul of his own.

Three Cats in One House

Our journey started on an August day many years ago. The litter was born in June, and a longer stay on the farm was undesirable. The two kittens were the only ones left, but I had in mind one cat for the house. My expectation was it would breathe freshness into my relationship with my husband because I believed in a saying: To be revitalized, your man needs a new car, a new house, or a new job. After purchasing a new house, one cat would be just fine. However, instead of one cat, we came home with both brothers to prevent the farmer from dumping the remaining kitten into the creek.

While back at home, we began arguing about how far should we restrict the kittens' freedom and what names to give to our new relatives. I thought our sunny yard was the perfect place for them to explore the world. My husband, as usual, had a different opinion. Such a place of freedom might be pregnant with diseases, he insisted, and I could immediately smell the breath of freshness. He imposed a veto: the kittens could explore the world through the glass patio door, dwelling in the living area as if in an aquarium. Thus those boys, after having two wonderful months on the farm, were incarcerated for the rest of their lives.

Choosing their names was not an easy task, either. Both kittens had green eyes and identical body architecture. Despite their plebian origin, they were the embodiment of elegance. One had a glossy black fur coat, tuxedo, with ornate snow-white collar and chest, short white gloves, and a tiny black spot on the tip of his otherwise white nose. The other kitten wore a gray coat with wild patterns of black rosette spots and strips, especially on his forelegs. The black capital letter "M" crowned its forehead, and horizontal, black strings alongside the corners of his eyes. This coat undoubtedly descended from a Bengal ancestor. They were cute and curious companions, and we had to observe them longer to name properly.

Within a few months, differences in their characters became obvious. Lounging in the sunshine next to the glass door, they followed every motion in the yard. Unlike the guy in the Bengal coat, the black kitten strived to partake in the life on the other side of the glass, as the audience of the first movie theaters who attempted to interfere with the actions on the screen. From behind the glass, this kitten tried to chase birds, following their impetuous flights. It rushed along a wall inside the house, from the patio door to the window in the corner of the room, and, tiptoeing, reached the glass. Shivering with every hair in his gorgeous coat, he hissed furiously. The birds, aware the hunter was in captivity, ignored him or even provoked his aggression. While this hunting fever went on, the other kitten stretched in the sun, leisurely observing his brother's vanity, a rather melancholic creature.

During a housewarming party, another occasion showed the cats' distinct personalities. After dinner my husband opened his guitar box on the rug in the living room and removed the guitar. The brothers immediately occupied the case, exploring every inch. No force was capable of pushing them out.

Nevertheless, as soon as my husband strummed the first musical chords, the melancholic twin froze on the red lining of the bottom of the case, staring at my husband, intrigued by never before heard sounds, his ears moving. Decisively, he turned away from his brother, jumped out of the case, and in two steps reached the musician. Approaching my husband from behind, he hopped on his shoulder and bent down to sniff the guitar's "hand." It seemed the "hand" was not what he was looking for, so he continued climbing along my husband's body, approaching the guitar from various angles. At last, he jumped to the floor and faced the front panel. Tiptoeing on his hind legs, he eventually put his curious nose into the sound hole and found the source of the sound. This task accomplished, the investigator took a place about five feet away among the audience.

This guy needs the name of an explorer or artist, I thought. But what about his brother, the hunter? Finally, after a discussion, we turned to French art and ended up with Cezanne and Matisse, the painters. The art connoisseur was Matisse the Thinker, also, for the pronounced capital "M" on its forehead. His brother in tuxedo became Cezanne the Hunter. Later Matisse surprised us with his special intellectual skills.

The brothers took over our house instantly. They were a perfect couple to exercise any Olympic sport. I used to get goose flesh when they leaped to the very top of a bookshelf where Chinese and Italian vases, wedding gifts, shone in their beauty. My efforts to restrict their athletic activities failed. Their free spirit cultivated during two months on the farm was remarkable. The kitchen counters were no different from the floor, and stealing food from dishes was common thing for those young bandits. The hunter, perhaps because of his martial inclinations, was easier disciplined than his bohemian brother.

From the first days in the house, the brothers showed great affection toward each other. They shared everything—the food, the bed, and the playground. Their fraternal love, however, did not stop them from engaging in occasional fights in the basement which we classified as martial arts. Matisse the Thinker never attacked first and always yielded to Cezanne the Hunter who usually appeared from the basement first, with his tail highly raised, and Matisse second, with a bleeding nose or patches of missing hair.

Once after a scuffle, Matisse materialized with shaggy hair all over his body. He took a position next to my chair and began grooming the sticking-out patches of his otherwise intact coat. When Cezanne emerged from the basement, I noticed a deep scratch above one of his eyes. Blood stained his white dicky. This time, his tail was down, and he looked puzzled. This incident was the end of Matisse's subjugation. Resisting Cezanne's bulling, he developed outstanding musculature and overcame his previously saintly tolerance.

Whenever I was resting on the sofa, Cezanne would climb onto my chest and stretch out his long and beautiful body, gaze into my eyes, sheathe his nails carefully, and occasionally knock at my chin. While we were indulged in our mutual affection, Matisse watched TV either sitting about three feet away from it or perching on its top. When he saw the TV for the first time, he started circling it, desperately searching for the source of the small figures dwelling on the screen. He would hit these creatures with his paw and then carefully inspect the paw. Nothing. Finally, he accepted TV people, perhaps understanding that knowledge has its limits.

On one occasion, I was lucky to observe his study of the law of cause and effect. Snuggled on the sofa, I knitted a scarf. A dim light from the window mixed with light from my lamp, brightened all the objects in the room. Cezanne, as usual, stared through the window, following a quarrel between crows. Matisse settled right in front of the TV. Although the TV was off, its screen reflected the entire room and provided the perception of depth. Fascinated by the screen, Matisse occasionally turned his head, then stared at the screen again.

Distracted by my thoughts, I dropped my ball of yarn. Matisse immediately glanced around, spotted the skein, and turned back to the TV screen, following the reflection of the ball as it rolled to the window where Cezanne sat. Ignoring the yarn, Cezanne audibly yawned. Matisse, staring at his brother's reflection, turned his head to the window to verify his observations. Bored by the still picture outside the window, Cezanne abandoned his outpost and absently crossed the room diagonally. Having noticed a moving cat on his display, Matisse turned back to see whether this was his brother. Confirming this fact, he continued his study session a good half an hour. Unlike Cezanne interested only in fauna, Matisse was an intellectual cat with great imagination.

I remember how weirdly he once started acting next to a closed closet door. Because I knew nothing animate could be inside—neither mice, nor bird, nor human—his prowling made no sense to me. I became concerned about his mental state as he writhed and flinched. When it went too far, I simply opened the closet door and let him in. He immediately recovered his senses.

It happened again, with a subtle variation. I left my black, woolen shawl on the corner couch in the living room. Entering the room, Matisse shied as soon as he noticed the item, the size of a big cat. Immediately, a dance of curious expectation began: prowling, lurking, sneaking, and smelling—I had seen it all before. It took him a full several minutes to cover the seven-foot distance to the couch. Only when he reached to the edge, sniffed, and carefully inspected the cloak, was he relieved.

Due to Matisse's open mind, he gradually got used to being groomed with our vacuum cleaner, while Cezanne ran headlong at the appearance of this noisy air-eating monster. It is hard to say how Matisse's talents might compensate for his lack of hunting instinct in the wild, but his exploratory skills were remarkable.

* * *

The third summer the brothers lived in our house, I developed strange, blisters—first on my hands, then on my ankles, and finally all over my body. None of my creams worked, and in a week I was in a doctor's office.

Having examined my hands, the doctor asked, "Have you worked in your garden recently?"

"Sure, I have weeded there. After each rain."

Making notes in my chart, he said firmly, "Poison ivy."

To tell the truth, I had only heard about this notorious plant but had never seen it. Perhaps my face expressed doubt, and the doctor came with help.

"Look for a vine, three leaves together."

"Vine? Yes, there was a vine. First, I pulled it, then cut with scissors, the same scissors I use in the house."

I looked at my fingers—all blistered, a mess of flesh—and immediately connected them to the scissors. Undoubtedly, I spread the toxin while poking hither and thither through the yard door. The next week after generous treatments of my fingers, I donned rubber gloves atop cotton ones and started the decontamination process. I washed each piece of cloth and each towel in use, every furniture item I had touched, each rug I stepped on, and all old linens. It was a busy summer. But how to decontaminate cats, I had no idea. While I spread the toxin around, the brothers were relaxing on a sunny spot on the carpet next to the door to the yard. As if lying in recliners, they stretched their hind legs far ahead on the floor and one of the front legs locked behind their heads as though in a yoga posture and obsessively groomed their fluffy bellies and private parts, which, I believed, had the traces of the deadly toxin.

A good washing would certainly do the trick. But how could I bathe them? These bastards avoided water religiously, disgustedly shaking the occasional accidental drop from their paws and their precious coats. My friends suggested using a bucket and soaking them in soapy water; it is always easier to give advice than to follow it. I knew how strong these lovely animals were and what weapons they carried, having never been declawed.

Yet I had to make the decision promptly; otherwise, my painstaking efforts to sterilize the house would fail. I developed a detailed plan. I would use two buckets; one with soapy water and another with clear; the bathtub would be the appropriate location for this sort of water boarding procedure. My personal protection was a particular issue—leather jacket, leather gloves, and the huge goggles I wore when mowing the lawn. The thought of a crash helmet also crossed my mind, but I quickly dismissed it.

After I had made the necessary preparations, I snatched the strongest cat, Cezanne the Hunter, and tucked him under my arm, and rushed to the torture chamber, trying to pet him gently on the way. Because my hands were less gentle than he was used to, he instantly suspected something. My heart, a beating drum against my chest, attempted to escape my chest, adding to the cat's panic, for Cezanne could feel it.

Holding Cezanne's upper body in a death grip, I struggled now to force him into the first bucket. The poor fellow had no idea about my good intentions. He probably thought it was the end of his world. He knew nothing about cats' nine lives: For three he plays, for three he strays, and for the last three he stays. Thus he fought ferociously. Tensing his muscular body, he propped his legs against the edges of the bucket so that I only managed to dip his private parts into the first bucket. A rinse was out of the question.

My mind was racing. Procrastination could be fatal, and I let my tight hold go. In a flash, Cezanne jerked like an uncoiled spring and shot out of the torture chamber. From a remote corner behind the bed, he let out a prolonged howl and then another. For a moment, I was paralyzed with terror. But there was still Matisse to deal with. The Thinker understood danger and hid quickly. Yet after a little thrashing, he got his shot, too.

Although the scene was now deserted of cats, Cezanne's howls could be heard in the neighborhood for an hour after my mission was accomplished. The humiliated felines licked the soap from their damp coats, and I hoped that the poison was at least partially dissolved. For a week the cats shunned me, but little by little the incident receded into their long-term memory, and trust was restored.

* * *

No longer a kitten, Matisse continued improving his exploration skills and now could easily open a screen door, a fragile gate between the house and the yard. I kept vigilant watch on the door lock he constantly tested. Once, when I left the screen unlatched, the bandits vanished. It was not a good sign, especially because I was expecting the return of my spouse, their patron, from a business trip.

As soon as I had connected all the dots, I slid down along the long flights of steps and rushed through the yard door, immediately spotting the guys. Intoxicated by their sudden freedom, they reached the very edge of our yard where my berry garden faced the hill. The wall of raspberry and gooseberry bushes halted their invasion of the neighbor's yard where birds, having escaped the encounter with the twins, perched on the lower branches of the trees.

Drumming his bared teeth, Cezanne was lost in hunting fever. He seemed in a trance, unable to run away. In the meantime, cunning Matisse who would always find the most secret, inaccessible hiding places squeezed through the thorny branches of the gooseberry bushes and hid there. To catch him, I knelt, my head toward the ground, and stretched my arm out as far as I could. When I felt his fur, I seized his hind leg and pulled it slightly. Matisse, unwilling to give up easily, screamed in despair as if sounding his final call before being incarcerated.

In the blink of an eye, his brother landed on my head and wrapped his muscular body around it. Grasping my forehead with his front paws and my neck and chin with the hind, he plowed through my scalp with his unsheathed claws, his lethal equipment. Where is my helmet, wondered my brain. Having finished disfiguring me, he landed onto the ground and froze next to my head. Matisse understood something odd had happened and retreated in the blink of an eye.

And here we were. My favorite cat had committed a misdemeanor. Having forgotten who I was and what we had in common, in a matter of seconds, Cezanne had released against me all the aggression intended for the birds mocking him from the trees. I felt his action was an impulse, a reaction to the shrilling call of Matisse. But couldn't it as likely be his revenge for my mistreatment, for the water torture? Actually I related to him, his failure to think before acting. My brain often took a similar detour, causing my own troubles.

While Cezanne stood stone-still, I slowly rose. Blood, streaming across my face, blinded my eyes. Glancing at the cat, I ordered, "Come on! Go!" and gestured him to the house and to the open patio door they had come through a few minutes ago in search of adventures. He obeyed me and went to the basement where I locked him in.

Moments later the front door opened, and our neighbor entered, holding Matisse in her arms. She glanced at me and muttered, "In Puerto Rico, my father would shoot such an offender." Fortunately for the cat, we were not in Puerto Rico! In the emergency room, the nurse applied one by one ten staples to my scalp, whispering, "Cats are known trouble makers, but this one did a good job on you."

Cezanne spent three days in the basement seemingly without any drive to socialize. When he eventually emerged, we kept a distance that diminished bit by bit until trust was completely restored. In a couple of months, spread like a sphinx along my body on the couch, his claws carefully sheathed, purring with delight, he could gaze into my eyes again. But this idyllic harmony was soon disrupted.

* * *

It happened closer to the winter when the days shrunk and it grew dark early. I had been shopping and was arriving back home. With one hand, I tried to unlock the door and with the other, I held my groceries. I desperately besieged the house, where on the stove I left a pot of simmering soup. I needed no more accidents. No more fingers in the mixer, oil burns, or poison ivy. Enough! Preoccupied with my worries, I suddenly felt a creature gently land on my lower back. Although I wore a thick drape coat, I could feel a squirrel-sized animal climbing to my shoulders. My first thought was that one of our cats escaped the house and was trying this clever trick to enter it again. But no, this was not their way; we had to chase our farm-born bastards to reclaim them. Besides, the creature was far too light compared to our grown up cats.

After eventually succeeding with my key, I slammed open the door and grabbed the creature from my back, only to discover a skinny little thing with long black fur and glowing eyes. "Oh, Jesus! Don't we have enough cats?"

Inside, raising their tails like exotic peacocks, the brothers welcomed me, cruising toward the entrance, but I had an uninvited guest in my hand. What should I do with this fragile thing? The stink of burning food instantly put an end to my hesitation. Dropping my load on the floor, I rushed to the stove. Right in time. The little bit of broth left in the pot barely covered chicken legs desperately begging for my attention. I quickly added water and hurried back to the entryway to pick up vegetables left there. Surprise! Without any invitation, the thing passed the astonished brothers as if they were just stone sphinxes and proceeded straight toward the kitchen.

When I re-entered the kitchen, I found it on the stove, trying to extract a chicken leg from the steaming soup. I pushed the invader away, but the kitten showed no willingness to obey. It climbed onto the kitchen counter again, this time leaving long scratches in the wood. Well, I thought, the soup could wait; this waif seemed on the verge of starvation.

I made a plate of cat food and, foreseeing arguments between the visitor and the brothers, placed the plate in the corner, next to the stove, for protection in case of emergency. As soon as our guest understood the food was served, it attacked the plate, devouring the meal and letting out threatening growls against any move within a nine-foot radius. Saliva streamed as the pellets disappeared in the kitten's mouth. Clearly, if any of the witnesses tried to interfere, a bloody battle would be unavoidable. If I did not know the little beast feasting was feline, I could have bet it were a dog.

Luckily, Cezanne and Matisse were real gentlemen. From a distance, they observed, configuring themselves into stately sitting postures—their tails tightly wrapped around their body. Only occasionally they exchanged superior, knowing glances with one another.

Shortly after my husband arrived. Curiously, he inspected the black fur ball that could easily fit into one of his palms. The question hanging like mist in the air was, what do we do now? Going around the neighborhood in the middle of the night, looking for someone missing a cat was not an attractive idea. And what if we wouldn't find this cat's home? I was hesitant to adopt a stranger with such plebeian habits. I had plenty of frustrations raising the brothers and had no desire to start all over again. With this musing in mind, I delivered my concerns together with the generously spiced chicken soup to the dining table.

My concerns, however, failed to convince my husband who was looking at the furry creature with admiration. As though encouraged by the attention received, it took a run and, barely overcoming force of gravity, landed on the table between the two steaming plates. Instantly, I grabbed the kitten's scruff and dropped it on the floor.

After dinner, I had a little time to inspect the newcomer and give it a bath. Sitting in the sink, dramatically shrunk in its wet and shiny suit, the creature curiously examined its image in the mirror. Neither of the brothers had shown an interest in their mirror reflections so far, and I thought this egotism spoke of the female nature of the kitten. When we eventually found ourselves in bed, a friend called. After getting familiar with the story, he warned us the cat would be killed in the shelter if it were not adopted after ten days.

The next day we made the rounds to the neighbors, but nobody claimed the emaciated feline. Some reported having seen a black kitten trying to enter their houses or cars the past month, so we decided to give a roof to this orphan.

From the beginning, she showed no interest in new step-brothers. She lived in the house as if she were the only cat there, an independent little thing. Our boys, on the other hand, were sociable animals, enjoying the company of each other and of our visitors; the little thing, however, ignored strangers. Thus, we called her The Thing.

The brothers, for good or ill, stayed at home under house arrest, though they rebelled periodically and tried to escape. Unlike the brothers, The Thing kept her distance from open doors, as though afraid of being expelled and homeless again. Although she was brave enough with the brothers and gradually developed trust in us, when plastic bags with their rustling sound appeared, she rushed headlong away. These bags were the nightmare that followed her for her entire life, and I wondered whether her original owners threw her out of their premises in a plastic bag.

The Thing matured quickly and in three months was a young attractive Maine Coon cat with silky flowing coat and long, bushy tail, undoubtedly emanating fragrances and expecting interest from our castrated brothers who paid no attention to her sexual appeal. Eventually, we fixed The Thing too, and the situation in the house re-stabilized. Her eating manner finally changed at the end of the first year when she became convinced of our sincere intentions and her permanent residency.

Promoting order in the house, I tried to impose restrictions on Thing's behavior, but as a real American, she rejected interference in her personal life, considering any such interventions an expression of socialism. A superior being, she eventually took complete control of the brothers and developed a close relationship with my husband.

When he was away for a week or more, her gorgeous fur became shaggy and lost its gloss, an unmistakable sign of depression.

Jealous of the brothers, she never allowed us to even pet her in their presence. While the brothers could share my husband's body, one on his lap and another on his shoulder, she had to have him only for herself. In fact, petting was performed only at her request, and to enjoy intimacy, she developed a trick.

A true hedonist, she loved her time in bed, especially our bed in the master bedroom on the second level. She would appear on the staircase above the living room on her way to the bedroom and make a couple of inviting calls. If my husband was sharing the company of the brothers under the balcony and did not respond or follow her, she would jump up on the wooden handrail and balance her body like an acrobat on a rope. If this performance were not enough to entice him, she would put two of her paws over the railing, threatening to jump from the twelve-foot height. Indeed, she did so several times. After those occasions, he always responded to her invitation. Thus the animal learned how to manipulate the man. She would not let him to take a single step on his own always following him, even to the bathroom.

Unlike the brothers waiting patiently during my husband's guitar lessons, The Thing would start biting his arm and striking calculated blows at the guitar.

When The Thing imposed her dictatorship, the master bedroom became a "forbidden city" for the brothers. If one of them appeared at the door, she furiously attacked and chased the victim down to the basement, growling and hissing. The patches of fur forfeited by the victim marked the path of humiliation. She rejected all territorial claims made by her cat housemates. On my returns from business trips, she tolerated my intrusion and reluctantly yielded the bed.

Thing's harassments would miraculously cease in summer, after her annual haircut, and she became a calm and shy green-eyed girl. I guessed her massive fur coat, at least two inches long, gave her outsized confidence. As soon as it went off, her petite body was exposed, humbling her. Her superiority was restored as soon as her coat grew long again.

Little by little—we could not recall exactly when and how it happened—The Thing learned to speak. Her satisfaction with our petting would be expressed by a gentle "*Uuurhaarr*. If petting was imposed on her, the answer was *uauauauuu*. Her threats sounded like *uuuurr*! Objecting petting, she wouldn't let us approach and her comment would be *wooow*! Passing her on the stairs, one would hear a guttural "*urh*" meaning, you again!

Thing could also issue silent orders. Sitting next to the kitchen sink meant she desired a gentle water stream. She would study a tiny water stream or a vortex on the bottom of the sink for hours, occasionally drinking from it. When we put a pot with water on the kitchen floor, she developed a habit of drinking water with her paw. Soaking the paw in the pot, she thoroughly licked the water from between her fingers. Whether she was imitating our spoons, it was hard to say, but she used the paw as a spoon only in the kitchen. Later, Matisse also adopted this drinking habit. Rectangular boxes from the refrigerator always invited her for milk. It was after serving her little milk that she gave me her first kiss

One more story remains to be told about this animal with the strong personality. It happened during the election of George W. Bush to a second term. The counting of ballots started in the evening, and I had no doubt the dark era was over as I prepared to celebrate victory. The Wheel of Fortune, however, screeched to a halt and pointed at George W., again, and America's map instantly blushed.

I was desperate! I could not imagine the sun would rise the next morning, but it did. Ignoring it, I stayed in bed. The Thing did not appear, either. The two of us lived alone after my husband moved with Cezanne and Matisse to Des Moines closer to the university where he was teaching. At first, after the sleepless night, I failed to notice the cat missing. When I began looking around the house, inspecting all its corners, I found nothing! No trace. I hadn't the courage to call my husband and deliver this devastating news. By that time I had become used to the truth—the cats, not me, were his priority.

All day I inspected the backyards in the neighborhood. A friend came to help, and we went to the lake, a half a mile away from the house, where wild life flourished. All our calls for the Thing, however, went on unanswered, and I imagined the worst possible scenario; she fell prey to a jackal. After hours of desperate searching, I was back in the house and decided on another maneuver before updating my husband on the unexpected development in our lives.

I put a cook pot on the stove and started preparing chicken soup. When the aroma of the soup saturated the house, I opened all windows and turned on the stereo speakers to the maximum. My favorite music escaped through the windows. A breeze instantly sent the depressing motives I was bathing in, and the fragrance of the chicken soup all the way to the lake. If the cat was in the northern part of town, I thought, she could not possibly miss the message.

Indeed, in about fifteen minutes, when a dramatic recitative between the musical passages started, I recognized a gentle mew from behind the window overlooking the porch. Thank Allah! The prodigal Thing was back, and I could release the classified information on the rebellion of the cat against The Electoral College. It was the only time she had run away, and I was perfectly aware of the reason.

UUUUUUUUUUUUUURRRRRRRRRRRRMMMM MMMMMMMM is the cryptic message I always find in my documents after leaving my laptop unattended briefly. Yes, despite her stubbornness, The Thing assists my writing. She often sits on a blank piece of paper ready for my notes, staring thoughtfully at it. After such pre-treatment, my thoughts stream faster and my writing firms up as though it is directed by an invisible script left by the cat and revealed only by my touch.

The Way Our Animals Love Us

It was one of those chilly days when the temperature dropped below minus thirty and humidity in the air was virtually non-existent. It seemed all water molecules froze out from the air to form picturesque white lace on the trees. Having approached the entrance door to our apartment building, I discovered the code in the electronic security box refused to work properly as it happened usually during spells of arctic chills. Luckily, our kitchen window overlooked the roof above the entryway. I grasped a snow lump from a glossy pile nearby and made a snowball. Taking a wide swing, I flung it toward the window. It hit the window sill and bounced off. Disintegrating in the air, it sent icy crystals into my eyes. The snow was too dry to stick. I took my mittens off, grasped two more handfuls of snow, and tried to make another ball, burning my hands.

In the twilight, I noticed a silhouette of a small animal, completely still, about ninety feet away, next to the garbage container. Occasionally cats would scavenge the garbage but not in such a deep freeze. I dropped the snowball and sprinted toward the container, one of my hands in my coat pocket, the other helping me keep balance on the slippery path.

Indeed, a black kitten like a statuette, its eyes closed, seemed frozen to the ground. I nudged it slightly, blowing my breath onto my hands, trying to warm them. In my peripheral vision, I saw the light came on in our kitchen window. I was about to hurry back to the building, when I realized the statuette had opened its glassy eyes. Without a second thought, I snatched up the little piece of animal life and raced back. Having dropped the black fur clod next to the door, I pulled on my mittens, grasped my snowballs and, one by one, threw them at the window. This time both reached their destination, knocking at the glass. My son, Roman (or Roma), drew the curtain, leaned toward the frosted glass, and opened the partition.

"Open the door," I yelled.

After I heard the lock click, I immediately pulled the door and put my foot on the threshold to prevent it from locking again. Twisting around, I picked up my grocery bags and the kitten and with my shoulder pushed the door wide open. Roman who had been begging for a dog was surprised to see a kitten instead.

"Look what I found! Put the poor thing in a shoe box on top of the heater. It may recover. Let's give it a shot." I took a quick look between the hind legs, "A girl," and rushed to the kitchen to prepare dinner. When I offered food, the kitty showed no interest, so I warmed milk and spooned it into her mouth. She still seemed in a coma.

The next morning, she had revived, and I asked my son, "What are we going to do?"

"Let it stay," he replied. He gave the kitten a stroke from her head to her tail. She turned toward him. "We'll call her Madonna, mom. Let her stay."

"Madonna." I recalled all those music videos he was constantly watching on TV, not appropriate for a seven-year-old boy. "Madonna is too long. Besides, I thought you

wanted a dog. Our apartment is too small to have both."
*And another baby I am carrying already for two months under
my heart.*

"We will talk about this later," he said with his father's
intonation, zipping his boots and heading off to school.

* * *

In a few days, my husband, Sasha (short for Alexander),
returned from his business trip. As soon as he saw the kitten,
he exclaimed, "Monya!" It sounded Jewish to me, but the
name stuck, and thus, Madonna was converted to Judaism.
The cat hesitated at the door frame, but then approached
Sasha and rubbed her arched back against his pants' leg.
Accepted, I thought.

Roman enjoyed the cat's company, though he treated
her not as a gentle female but a tomboy. Or perhaps a
puppy, as he insisted on playing fetch with her. Although
Monya liked playing with the ball, she was reluctant to
advance her football skills. Nevertheless, Roman persisted,
especially after watching the Moscow Circus of Durov
whose animals, including cats, performed fantastic stunts.
Monya, alarmed by the increasing level of complexity
involved, went underground, hiding from him for hours.

At last, he let the feline alone, concluding she had
no performing skills. However, after enduring math and
zoology classes, Roman decided to observe the feline
closer, claiming her development was lagging. To prove his
point, he started a diary. Every week, he flattened the cat
on the floor and took her measurements. Monya objected,
expressing her opinion clearly—hissing and boxing at him,
occasionally unsheathing her claws.

* * *

Gradually Monya developed the habit of sleeping on my pregnant belly. Although I had no objections, my friends prophesied doom: "A cat sleeping on the belly leaves a stain, a birthmark on the baby's skin." Yet I didn't have the heart to push her away and lived in anxiety through the rest of my pregnancy. After the baby came, the very first question I asked the nurse was whether my daughter's skin was unblemished. "Snow-white," she replied.

Things changed after Nastya's birth. With a sister now, my son turned his interest toward a new subject, a human one this time. When we brought Nastya home, I unwrapped her on the table in the living room. Everyone approached to have a look, but Monya was first. Her hind paws on the chair, she propped the front ones on the edge of the table. Having stretched toward the baby, she took a sniff. At her attempt to make a contact, Sasha cut her short, "No!" Monya turned around, jumped from the chair, and abandoned the scene.

After introductions were over, Nastya closed her eyes, demonstrating her willingness to rest. I put her in the cart we used for her bed at the time and went to the kitchen to fix a snack for myself. It was nearly time to nurse her. In about twenty minutes, Nastya cried, and I hurried back to her only to discover Monya on the bed, administering massage. She was gently tapping Nastya's legs, her eyes fixed on the baby as if checking her reaction.

In two giant steps, I reached the cart, grabbed the cat by its withers, and dropped her on the floor. "Enough, chiropractor! You may go now." Monya showed no intention to leave. Instead, she jumped back into the cart and observed me nursing. After I finished with Nastya,

I reprimanded Monya, "You shouldn't do that! Don't forget!" The cat rubbed against my leg, and I thought we had a deal. Wishful thinking. It became clear soon this cat was determined to adopt my daughter. No matter where she was, as soon as she heard Nastya's call, Monya flew to her headlong, always the first to reach the bed. Finally, I surrendered, accepting Monya's determination to lend a helping paw.

Monya was not only a caring nanny but also an excellent guard. When Nastya was only four months old, she caught a bug and developed cold symptoms. I called the pediatrician. As soon as Monya heard the doorbell ring, she shot to the bedroom. I opened the apartment door, let the doctor warm herself, and I ushered her to Nastya.

At the sight of Monya, the doctor gasped. "How can you allow this? Aren't you afraid for the baby?"

Monya was in the bed next to Nastya, her eyes challenging the doctor.

"No, I'm not," I replied. I waved the cat away and closed the bedroom door.

After the doctor had finished examining Nastya and gave her recommendations, I opened the door and discovered Monya waiting on the threshold. Immediately the cat rushed to the front door and jumped on a footstool under a coat stand, and started sending her well calculated strikes at the doctor's winter boots, while the doctor was putting her coat on.

* * *

Assisted by her nanny, Nastya quickly mastered crawling. They both would appear in tandem—first, Monya, then

Nastya. One day, the couple arrived in the kitchen, where I was fixing breakfast and simultaneously trying to finish the laundry. Having noticed the approaching procession, I stepped into the adjacent bathroom to drop the last load into the washer. Back in the kitchen, I was taken aback by what I saw: Nastya, on all fours, eating kibble from the cat's dish. And Monya, proud of her training skills, wrapping her elegant tail around her small body, observed the baby as she ate. I realized it was not the first meal they shared. Fortunately there were no side effects from this KitKat enriched menu. Nastya was developing normally, without paws or claws.

Following Monya's example, perhaps, Nastya refused to wear clothes at home until she learned how to put her pants on by herself. These two always dwelled naked within the walls of our apartment. As all normal cats do, our feline needed many naps during the day time. In vain we attempted to explain to Nastya the difference in the physiology of sleep between humans and cats. Sometimes, to keep Monya from her naps, Nastya simply threw the cat's tiny body over her shoulder or arm and continued her usual errands. Poor Monya never objected, obediently accepting her fate, but I did wonder if sleep deprivation was the reason she started destroying the internet cable. It impacted our modest budget, not to mention inconveniences for my mother, who during those tough times, could not reach us from abroad.

Unlike most cats, Monya enjoyed water. When one of us was in the bath, she perched on the edge of the tub, meditating. Occasionally she would even jump into the water herself. As far as Monya's drinking is concerned, she preferred running water to vodka, diverging from most Russians in this delicate matter.

Somehow my daughter and her nanny always understood each other, though neither spoke the other's language. While Monya knew just one word, "meow," with a dozen intonations, Nastya employed only one syllable, "mo." Her first real phrase was: "Monya, *mogie*!" She couldn't yet manage three syllables: *po-mo-gie* (help). No matter how busy Nanny Monya was when occupied with her own business, she would abandon everything to rescue Nastya.

Reprimanding Monya was my husband's responsibility. In his deep baritone, he would make clear his dissatisfaction, and despite her feline stubbornness, his lectures seemed worked. For instance, after his ban on dwelling on the tables, Monya gave up this idea. Of course, she heard about cats' liberties abroad that leaked through the Iron Curtain, but those were cats of imperialists. Monya was a Russian cat from a working family.

* * *

After the collapse of the Soviet Union, conditions in the country deteriorated rapidly. The effort of the Russian government to import democracy from the United States failed. The US wanted to sell us everything (including yogurt and "Bush Wings," as Russians christened American chicken's limbs) except democracy. People lost their jobs. University professors collected cigar butts in the streets, and my husband Sasha could no longer feed us with his photography. He carpentered for a number of years, making kitchen furniture in our garage without any ventilation.

Because this work brought only little money, Sasha assembled a team of laborers and went to Moscow, four hours away by plane, to build housing for "New Russians," finalizing the interiors of their luxurious apartments. He had the flu when they departed. The crew lived in the same apartments they worked on, inhaling all sorts of dust and toxic paints. When Sasha came back a few months later, I barely recognized him in the man I saw. He had dark circles under his eyes, gray skin on his face, his entire body seemed as if it had shrunk; he'd also become weak. With difficulty, he tried to continue working here and there, but during one of those trials, he broke his back and became bedridden. So now our family of four, plus cat Monya, depended only on my mother's support from abroad.

After a battery of tests, Sasha was diagnosed with the third stage of multiple myeloma cancer. Years of working with wood dust, formaldehyde, and other hazardous chemicals with no protection came to fruition. Bone resorption proceeded faster than bone reconstruction. Radiation and two rounds of chemo therapy were performed with poor results.

* * *

"Here we are!" Roma announced as soon as we entered the corridor of our apartment. Kicking off his boots, he proceeded straight to his father, and Nastya followed him.

"Give him to me," I heard Sasha saying. I rushed to assist, but Roma was already showing his ill father the Cocker Spaniel puppy, displaying all his body parts. Suddenly I realized how quickly my son had matured. At twelve, he was caring and thoughtful.

"Welcome," my husband said, tousling the puppy's silky ears. "My name is Alexander, but you may call me Sasha. And what is your name?"

"Boss is his name," Nastya replied for the puppy.

Instead of entering the conversation, Boss yawned and licked Sasha's hand.

"Sleepy devil." Roma laid the puppy on his father's belly. I pushed the kids back to the corridor to take off their coats. When I peeped back into the room, I saw Sasha wiping tears from his face as Boss nosed his frail body, even further diminished during the last months in bed. At this point, Monya appeared in the room. She and Nastya were six now. The cat prowled cautiously toward the bed, straightened her tail, put her front paws on the mattress, and took a sniff. After a moment, she turned her head to where I still was observing the scene at a distance.

"This is your little brother, Monya. Love him. He's a good boy," I said.

As though she needed to think this matter over and could do so better behind closed doors, Monya quietly removed herself from the room. The next day she decided to ignore Boss.

After dinner, we transformed a box from my sewing machine into a bed for Boss and put down a towel that Maxim, the puppy's previous owner and veterinarian, had given to me. It smelled of Boss's mother. No success. The entire night, Boss whimpered, searching the corners of the apartment for his lost family. The second night was no different, and Roma took the puppy in his bed. Comfortably nestled on the blanket, at last Boss slept soundly through the night.

From the beginning, we noted that when lying on the floor, Boss extended his hind legs behind him like a furry frog. I had never seen a posture like this in dogs. Worrying something was wrong with his hip joints, I called Maxim who reassured me: "Nothing is wrong unless this is hip dysplasia, but he is fine."

The next two months passed without any animal incidents except for Boss's determination to mark every inch of our apartment. Perhaps he was trying to expropriate the territory from Monya, yet Monya remained silent. Then we noticed Boss taking over her toys. Catching him in the act, we would tell him, "Leave it!" Reluctantly he spat out a mouse or a fish, but even Monya's ball was eventually transferred to Boss, though he had his own. Monya still didn't complain.

Training Boss was Sasha's prerogative. I also relied on him now to tutor the kids, so his mind would be constantly busy. Often the kids would deliver Boss on the carpet next to Sasha's bed together with a disputed article and order Boss, "Sit." And Sasha would start, "Boss, look what huge ears you have." Boss would shake his floppy, shoulder-length ears, staring at Sasha with his bottomless innocent eyes. "If you touch Nastya's slippers again," he shook it before Boss's nose, "I'll pull your ears." The dog would arch his brows, one and then the other, frown, wrinkling the crown of his head, as if thinking over the message, and turn away his head to escape his master's gaze. To this, Sasha would say, "Dismissed," after which Boss shot headlong out of the room and collided with the kids, eavesdropping next to the door and chuckling.

* * *

Boss was about five months old when he suddenly showed signs of apathy—no interest in communication, in play, or food. Acting as a nurse and caregiver to Sasha, being the liaison with all the doctors, plus all the work at home and with the kids, I had no time to worry about Boss's morale. We all have blues, I thought. But the next day things got worse: high fever, vomiting, and then diarrhea—all at the same time. Immediately I called the veterinarian and described his symptoms.

"Enteritis," Maxim cut me short, "an inflammation of the small intestine."

"How did he get it?"

"Oh! Parasites, bacteria, viruses. Look out the window. See the puddles of dirty water. The snow has thawed, and all sorts of shit is in there."

Listening to him, I was hectically calculating the chances the kids or Sasha could catch enteritis from Boss. "Is he contagious?"

"Not to humans. To animals, rarely."

"And what is the prognosis?"

"The prognosis on average is good but not for puppies. Dehydration and secondary infections are the grand killers, and the treatment is complex, especially at home. And there are no hospitals, not even enough for people, as you probably know."

"I'm painfully aware."

"Sorry."

"What can I do? What would you do if this were your dog? I am a nurse after all."

After a pause, Maxim gave me the list of prescriptions, "He will need special serum to prevent virus reproduction, two antibiotics to prevent secondary infections, immunomodulators, glucose, and vitamins. Eight or ten injections daily."

I whistled, thinking of the cost.

"But I want to warn you that he's probably going to die anyway, considering his current condition."

Nastya listened carefully to the conversation. As soon as I put the receiver down, she asked, "Mom, we aren't going to let him die?"

I hugged her shoulder. "We'll try our best."

"Lena, let me look at him," Sasha called from the bed.

I wrapped Boss into his favorite towel and brought him to Sasha. "Come on, buddy! Don't even think about dying before me." He twisted Boss's ears and let us go.

Luckily, our neighborhood pharmacy had everything I needed. Bustling around, I stowed Boss's medications on a separate shelf in the kitchen. I must be careful not to mix them with Sasha's spasmolytics and morphine. One can never be too careful, I thought. As the vet suggested, I gave Boss his eight injections daily, and Nastya always observed me, patting him. Boss, however, showed no reaction, not even a blink, his eyes always closed. Having stopped eating and drinking, in just a couple of days, he lost all his former cuteness. A sack of bones, a stinky, shaky skeleton, with bloody discharge and tarry feces spread on his rug, he slowly faded.

The kids continued to love him; they patted his tormented body and talked encouragingly. Occasionally I would take him to Sasha. "What is going on, buddy? What did you decide? To live or to die? It's all on you," Sasha would murmur.

Once, I caught Nastya in the kids' room, whispering next to the window sill where she built a home for her dolls.

"Who you are talking to?" I asked concerned.

"To God," she mumbled.

"To God? Do you believe in God?"

"I don't know yet."

"And what are you talking about?"

"About Papa and about Boss." Nastya shyly turned her head, tears making their way down to her chin. I reached and embraced her. "Don't worry. They will be fine." I pushed back my own sobbing. *I never cry.*

The third week, when I approached Boss with the syringe and attempted to find a good spot, pressing his body through shaggy hair that had lost its gloss, he snarled at me.

"Wow! Revived. Okay. Let's go to the kitchen." I walked to the kitchen and began to heat some chicken soup.

In a few minutes, Boss crawled through the doorway, and I began to spoon the soup into his mouth. Sasha seemed to understand what was going on and called Boss. I doubted the poor fellow could make it to the bedroom on his own, so I wrapped him in the towel and brought him to Sasha.

"So what, you bastard? You've survived? Now you have to live a long life and be fearless. Protect my kids from those bullies—fighter dogs. Where did all these breeds come from, Boss? Cordoba, Kangal, Kuchi—all those beauties of capitalism. Look at what happened to our neighborhood." Boss had no answers to these difficult questions. It seemed those bullies arrived together with "New Russians."

As soon as Boss's began to recover, he devoured his meals, his golden beauty gradually returning. One day, he was sitting next to the chair, where I had placed Sasha's meal. Roma, feeding Sasha, also tried to follow the action on the TV screen, far in the corner. After providing a bite to Sasha, he turned his head away. At this moment, Boss stole a piece of chicken from the plate. Sasha wiggled his finger at Boss and expressed himself clearly, using adjectives. And we thought the case was closed.

The next day, I brought Sasha a bowl of cholodez (jelly-like broth with meat) with some Russian mustard on the side, a really hot one. The cholodez wiggled when I was cutting it into small pieces. After cutting, I topped it generously with mustard. Boss observed the process with great interest, tilting his head thoughtfully. Clearly, the shaking of the *cholodez* puzzled him. As soon as I started moving the fork along the familiar trajectory, toward Sasha's mouth, Boss intercepted the portion. Before anyone could react, he swallowed it. Immediately, his shock was obvious. Boss's unblinking eyes teared, but he did not move from the spot, ready to humbly accept his punishment. Instead, I gave him a hug, laughing. The poor fellow was just trying to build up his strength lost in the battle for life.

* * *

In September, Nastya started elementary school, and during the morning hours, when I needed to run to the clinic or hospital, the market or pharmacy, I used to leave Sasha alone with the pets. Back at home, I occasionally would find Boss's poop or Monya's hairball on Sasha's blanket. "Wife, these are natural attributes of life. Don't complain," Sasha would say.

But once I found an assembly meeting on Sasha's bed—Monya half-sitting at the foot of the bed, Nastya next to her, holding her hand on the cat's pregnant belly, Boss resting his head on the mattress. Monya generally got pregnant while on vacation in the camping ground, and this year was no different.

"What's going on here?" I asked, surprised to see something like a roadside picnic.

"We are giving birth," Sasha replied. An hour later Monya delivered two kittens without complications, one of them a giant.

Every once in a while, in the sickroom I would catch snippets of Sasha's talking to Boss. He told Boss the things he concealed from me. "What a pain when every bone falls apart! There are two hundreds and six of them. The spinal cord is a bridge, buddy. No bridge, no communication. That's how it works." Entering the room, I would find Boss either sitting on the floor or supine in bed beside Sasha, his front paws thrown far behind his head and the hind ones spread like in human. What a strange couple! They traveled together but in the opposite direction. While Sasha's shrinking body barely supported his stoic spirits, Boss's exuberant body contained a promise for a long life and comfort to all of us.

The little dog somehow knew his master had a special need for love, and he gave it unconditionally. While I watched them, Boss opened one of his sad eyes and gazed at me as if trying to read my thoughts. The nature of this mind-reading ability always puzzled me. Then, as though he had understood, he sighed and turned on his side, snuggling around Sasha's shoulder, his little black nose nuzzled into Sasha's neck.

* * *

Sasha steadily approached his finale. The third dose of chemo therapy, which I had to administer at home, made things worse. Pain attacks became more frequent, and I feared morphine would not help much longer. The last five days, he was in agony, his arms rigid at his sides. I was perching on the edge of the bed when Boss joined me. He hopped up and began licking Sasha's hand. Sasha opened his eyes, and they stared at each other for a long while. When Sasha blacked out again, Boss jumped off the bed and sat on his haunches in the door frame, looking sadly and thoughtfully at Sasha. After he left the room, Monya showed up. She spent a half an hour at the same spot, gazing at us. That night Sasha was gone. None of the animals came back in the room after they bid goodbye to Sasha, not even when his body was removed.

* * *

When Boss was a puppy, the kids would say, "Go to Sasha. Show him your ears," and Boss would obey. About a year after Sasha's death, Roma had friends over, and Boss would not leave them alone. Remembering the old trick, Roma, said, "Go to Sasha. Show him your ears." Boss raised one of his brows, then another one as if in surprise, and raced to the bedroom where I was sorting clothes. He glanced at me, gave a startled yelp, and dashed back. This time he did not try to get the boys' attention. He simply took a place in the corner and eyed them with reproach. This was where I found him.

* * *

As an adult dog, Boss was a brave fellow, fearlessly chasing away packs of stray dogs, their tails between their legs, if they happened to trespass into his territory or approach family belongings left under his supervision. But the fighter dogs, wearing neither collar nor leash, enjoying the liberties of our young, unregulated capitalism, tended to produce terror in Boss and me. One of them, Oligarch, developed a habit of attacking him. Fully grown, Boss could fit under the belly of that bully. The attacker, with the bold, muscular body of a predator, wrinkling in bullying fever, would freeze above Boss and wait for his move. Boss, in turn, stood still, his eyes full of animal fear, waiting for us to rescue him. He knew one wrong move and he would be torn apart.

Boss was six when I first encountered a big dog closely while on vacation in summer. For drinking water, we used to go to the well outside the territory of our camping ground, passing a one-man house with a dog off leash. From a distance, I could see its red coat and impressive dimensions. He would sit beside the door and follow me intently with his eyes as if taking aim at me. Just the size of him made me anxious.

One day, a grocery kiosk stopped at our camp, and I had replenished our reserves. When I was about to leave, another shopper, his mane full of silver, introduced himself, "Oleg," and offered me a hand with my groceries.

"Lena," I replied, gazing into his smiling eyes. "I must have seen you somewhere around here?"

"Sure."

"But where?"

"You pass my house on your way to the well."

"With a big dog?" I felt relieved he was not a complete stranger.

He nodded. "Mensch is his name. He's not a barker, and he doesn't bite."

"Mensch? An unusual name for a dog. Mensch means human in German, yes?"

"A real human. Arian. Didn't we study German in schools? I still remember playing war games in the fifties after the war: *Halt! Hände hoch!*"

At this point, we reached a fork in the path, and I took my bags. "Thanks, and send my greetings to Mensch."

"*Auf wiedesehen*," Oleg replied in German. "By the way, my house has water pipe from the well, and you're welcome to use it."

Politely I declined his offer with the reference to his dog, and he receded in the twilight. Since that day onward, I frequently saw him next to his house as I walked to the well. Once when it rained for three days and we spent all our time inside, I found a bucket of clear water on our porch covered with a lid. "From Mensch," a note tied to it said.

When I finally visited Oleg in his little house, the dog simply approached me, made a couple of circles around me, and sniffed cautiously as if afraid to offend me with his attention. His thickly furred coat and tail were red as a fox's. His nose, muzzle, and a large fur collar were white as well as the lower section of his legs that looked as if he wore gloves. His erect, triangular ears moved, one at a time, easily tuning toward one's voice. He was a beautiful specimen.

"He could be a Siberian Husky, but red hair . . ."

To this, Mensch turned a one-eighty, left the house, and threw his bones down next to the entrance.

"No idea of his breed, if any. Some say he looks exactly like an Amur Husky," Oleg said, fixing his eyes on me.

"Never have seen that kind of Husky."

After that first meeting, I began stopping frequently at Oleg's place to have a cup of tea and enjoy small talk. Mensch always met me far away from the house, and I wondered how he knew I was coming. Wagging his fluffy golden tail, he escorted me both to Oleg's door and back to the fork in the road. Oleg, discharged from the Afghan war because of shell-shock, for many years worked as a guard for a neighbor's vacation resort. Divorced, he had an adult daughter living in the city, and fishing was his only pastime. At least, that was what I thought until I found out about his drinking.

Sometimes Oleg invited me to fish with him on his boat. Returning, we would find Mensch sprinting back and forth along the waterfront, barking, welcoming us back. During the next step of his reception ceremony, he propped his front paws against Oleg's chest so that their faces were on one level and gazed into his master's eyes. After licking Oleg's face, he usually tried to poke his massive head under Oleg's arm. This latter ritual seemed to me a request for a preliminary pardon because after that Mensch would run to me and convoy us to the house, always on my side, his tail wagging. The idea of propping his paws on my chest occurred to him once, but he never fulfilled it. Perhaps he knew it wouldn't be an appropriate gesture with a lady.

* * *

My kids had grown up. Nastya was already eleven and Roma seventeen. The one-room cabin we rented from the university summer camp became too small to accommodate the entire family—with the cat and the dog—and occasionally my father who used to come fishing. When the economy improved and science got money back, my father was able to build a large log cabin for us. The only lot available was across from Oleg's house, a hundred yards away from it.

The next summer, Nastya, Roma, and I, along with Boss and the cat, Monya, moved into the cabin although it was still unfinished. Our brand new place had neither water nor electricity yet, so we relied on Oleg's generosity. When he traveled to the city, he kindly left the key from his house so I wouldn't need to go to the well. The day we arrived, Oleg was away. After lunch the kids went to the beach, and I collected all the dirty dishes, a teapot, and a small bucket and headed to Oleg's place. Boss expressed interest in going with me, but I made him stay on the porch—to guard the cabin. Besides, he had not yet been introduced to Mensch.

An hour later, I exited Oleg's house and was greeted by the big dog who appeared from nowhere. Holding in one hand the teapot full of hot water and in another the bucket of clean dishes, I was on my way home, sensing the soft steps of Mensch behind me. Suddenly, I heard a rumbling growl and a sound as though heavy sacks of sand were collapsing on the ground. I jerked around, bewildered. A huge golden-red hairball rolled toward me. The dogs were brawling in the grass, their jaws locked. Boss, inferior in size, fought to protect his mistress like an audacious little knight. Impulsively, I almost poured the water onto the rolling ball to break up the fight but realized in time I had just boiled it.

"Stop it!" I blurted out and threw the teapot aside. I rushed toward the beasts and hit their heads with my fist, one and then the other. The dogs, dumbfounded by blows from the sky, instantly unlocked their embrace and sat up on their haunches, looking at me, panting, their tongues out.

"Never again! Do you hear me, Boss? Do you hear me, Mensch? Never again!" I displayed my fist to be sure they understood. Furiously, I grabbed my bucket and headed to the cabin. A few yards farther along, I stole a look back. The combatants were still motionless in the same posture, thinking over their future life without war.

After their militant introduction, the dogs became inseparable; for entertainment, they raced together around the neighborhood. Occasionally Mensch invited Boss hunting, though we were unsure what the role our dog played, or to dog courtships where Boss served simply as best man to Mensch, from a distance. And, of course, they worked as a team guarding the cabin. Our cabin.

I believed Mensch never neglected the safety of Oleg's house, but he guarded it from afar, now. From time to time, Oleg reminded him who was who, and Mensch would return to his place of residence but only for a while. He had two jobs nowadays and two masters. One of them, he cared about because of love and the other because of responsibility.

The introduction of Mensch to our cat, Monya, is also worth mentioning. Facing Mensch for the first time, she simply slapped his muzzle. Mensch, unused to such disrespect, bared his fangs and glanced at me. "No! Don't you dare!" I wiggled my finger next to his nose. Mensch sighed and with regret turned away. He put his head on his front paws and sank into daydreams, fantasizing about times when he would chase this little devil and show her the place in the hierarchy.

Speaking of Monya, once a stranger dog invaded our territory, and Mensch immediately made a move. Before he managed to even bark, however, the cat uncoiled like a spring and cut their communication short, positioning herself between the dogs, the fur on her arched back lifted, her tail ruffed. In a flash, the stranger was gone.

The university camping ground had a small café on the beach, and Nastya used to go there to hang around with her friends. Her arrival was always special, for she led a court. Mensch, wearing his face of extraordinary nobility, headed the procession. Boss, in his royal Cocker Spaniel apparel, followed him with dignity, and Monya brought up the rear, her tail raised up in triumph.

One night, when Nastya went to a discotheque with two other girls, she ordered Mensch to stay at home. Entering the woods, she heard labored breathing behind. Two eyes rushed toward them in the mysterious moonlight. Mensch decided the girls were more important than dozing with Boss on the porch, and he abandoned his outpost. Nastya tried to make him go back home. In vain. During the discotheque he stayed outdoors, only occasionally entering the hall to locate Nastya and then recede into the darkness behind the shelter again.

I remember observing Mensch in the line of duty. A team of young men worked outside on the water line while I was in the cabin. I made all preparations for cooking and needed to open a gas cylinder installed in my absence. Having no experience, I called one of the athletes to help. He entered, showed me the procedure, and turned to leave. A moment later, I heard his mournful: "Lena, help!" Glancing his way, I saw his wrist in Mensch's jaw, his eyes full of terror. "Let him go!" I ordered. Mensch cold-bloodedly released the prisoner, taking the observer position on the porch, his eyes lazily scanning the workers. It seemed I hurt Mensch's feelings. He didn't bite the man, after all, he simply halted him for further investigation, clutching his hand as if locked into handcuff. I stepped outside, patted his back, and ran my fingers through his thick mane.

At the beginning of our relationship, Mensch took his meals at Oleg's house. But since he spent more and more time at our place, I felt it was my duty to feed him together with my other animals. To tell the truth, the demand for food was higher than I could easily afford. The regular menu included kasha I cooked daily for them and occasionally a sausage stuffed with sub-products. When the feeding hour approached, the dogs gathered next to the porch. Mensch, the elder, was the first to be served, then Boss.

After the meal, there was always a siesta on the porch. At night, the kids and dogs slept in the attic, and there were constant arguments who was going to sleep with Boss. Mensch, of course, was far too big to sleep with anybody, so he retired on the floor. When I was around, he started

57

the night on the floor next to my bed, and in the morning I would find him in a half-and-half position, head and his front paws on my bed and his hindquarters on the floor. Awakening with me, he would start rubbing his sleepy eyes.

Once during a stormy night, when the thunder rolled over the house, I suddenly awoke feeling somebody next to me in bed pressing against my back. I stealthily explored the intruder. This was Mensch, hiding from the thunder.

Boss, on the other hand, feared fireworks. Knowing his Achilles's heel, we always took precautions during New Year's nights in the city, wrapping his head with scarves and sitting with him through the night as if at a wake. Once, when I delayed, and the first cannonade of fireworks exploded, Boss shot to the bathroom and squeezed into a far corner under the bathtub. There was no getting him out. Early the next morning, he materialized.

I always wondered how Mensch was able to keep his paws so meticulously clean. Of course, as soon as he moved over to our cabin, Nastya began grooming him together with Boss—shampooing, brushing, hugging, and kissing. This labor dog who used to sleep outdoors never before knew a tender touch. Only during cold spells in winter, did Oleg allow him to sleep in the cold corridor on top of sheep skins. And here suddenly all these trifles and luxuries, with the exception of pedicure perhaps.

After a light breakfast, when the sun shone invitingly, we enjoyed a couple of hours of sunbathing. When I was in the chaise lounge next to the cabin, the dogs would approach and wait, gazing into my eyes, unsure what spot to take. "Hide under the chaise-lounge," I would say, and obediently they dived under. On the beach, Boss would hang around, wagging his tail and his entire body, making peace with all Nastya's friends. Mensch, on the other hand, stayed with me, pressing his furry self against my body, his big head on my knees. The weather was hot enough without this overcoat, and I would ask him to go. With a canine sound of dissatisfaction, he moved a foot away but never left, subjecting himself to the tortuous heat in order to be nearby.

Kids used to mock him: "Mensch is in love." Indeed, he was. For the first time. Yet he never imposed himself. He merely served. I remember Oleg and I attended a bonfire dedicated to the opening of a new season at a neighboring camp. At about midnight, Mensch arrived. The crowd was under the influence of alcohol, and he should have stayed at home, guarding there. Oleg, swinging a beer bottle at Mensch, ordered, "Go home!" Mensch hung his head and went away, but a few minutes later appeared again, his eyes guilty. "Didn't I tell you to go home?" Oleg roared.

Mensch consulted me, but I didn't want to interfere. Although drunk, Oleg was his master. After a minute of procrastination, Mensch left.

"Why do you do this to him? You know how anxious he is when you're drunk." I swallowed hard, feeling for the dog and for myself.

"Anxious for you, not for me," Oleg stated drily.

"That's why you don't want him to stay? It's all over soon, and we could leave together."

About ten minutes later, Mensch showed up again and stood next to me. "Go home, Mensch! You'll be punished." Oleg continued to exercise his master's right. However, Mensch was not one to accept no for an answer. Having made a few steps out of the light circle, he crouched on the ground and started crawling, toward me. I couldn't play indifference any longer and made a move in his direction, meeting his hot breath on my chest. I kissed his handsome muzzle and whispered in his erect ear, "We never cry."

* * *

As with all hunting, Mensch's excursions into the wild were risky enterprises, and it looked as if his years of steady luck were behind him. At fourteen, he was still active, but his legs, affected by arthritis, occasionally refused to serve him properly. He couldn't climb the stairs to the porch, let alone the fifteen steep stairs to the attic, so somebody had to always assist him.

For four years every summer, he was with us, plus all those short weekends during other seasons when weather permitted. It was on one of those weekends when he disappeared for several hours. When he returned, we didn't recognize him. His noble face was mutilated; his cheek, torn from the jaw, hung freely, bleeding. I tried to disinfect it, but he wouldn't let me approach. He needed surgery, and Oleg promised to call the vet first thing the next morning, on Monday. I left for the city that evening.

The next Friday at noon I came back. I was unpacking, when I heard scratching on the door. I pushed it open, and the reek of rotting flesh hit my nose. I gasped. The detached piece of flesh, now a dark color, was still hanging in place.

"Mensch! Oh, dear!" I bent to the dog.

"Here we are," Oleg announced himself, entering our place.

I was furious. "Why didn't you call the vet? Mensch is rotting alive!"

"After it dries out, I will cut it with scissors."

"You're crazy! With scissors. You'll kill the dog. I'll call to the vet. Right now."

"Ask about the cost. I am short of cash." He took a seat.

I called my veterinarian friend Maxim and explained the emergency. He promised to come late in the afternoon, after all his other appointments, almost a two-hour drive from the city. His estimate for the surgery was six thousand rubles. Oleg had only three, so I promised to add the rest from Nastya's monthly pension of seven thousand she received from the government as a compensation for the death of her father.

Three hours passed, and we made all the preparations. Nastya and I cleaned the house. Oleg hewed a few pine planks and made an operating table. Maxim showed up in the twilight, when we had already lost hope he would come. Immediately he checked the dog. "A little too late," he regretted. "If you had called me at once, this flesh could be sewn to the jaw. Now, it can't. I should cut it off. There will be a permanent grin." His eyes met Oleg's.

"Who cares?" I interfered. "As long as the wound heals!"

"Then let's hurry." He glanced at his watch.

Maxim opened his leather bag, pulled out his instruments, and arranged the sterile packages on the table. From the car, he brought a surgical lamp. When everything was ready, he filled a syringe with sedative and approached Mensch laying on the rug. Mensch growled, baring his fangs.

Maxim handed the syringe to Oleg. "Do it yourself."

Oleg grabbed the syringe and made the injection, and in a few minutes Mensch relaxed, allowing Maxim to anesthetize him. The operation lasted about forty minutes. Maxim was still collecting his equipment when Mensch woke up. He rose and unsteadily headed toward the door. Nastya helped him down from the porch. Once back in the cabin, he dropped onto his rug and slept till morning. I spent the weekend chasing him with a bottle of hydrogen peroxide, attempting to disinfect the stitches.

After the operation, Mensch's face had indeed been distorted into a perpetual grin, and the kids renamed him "The Mensch Who Laughs."

* * *

The winter was unusually cold. For the second month in a row the temperature was stuck at minus 30. Most days schools were canceled, and kids stayed at home. We thought about going to our vacation cabin, but in this ringing frost . . .

Oleg didn't reply to my phone calls, so I didn't know what was going on with him, with his dog, or with our cabin, under his supervision. With his drinking, one could expect anything. Eventually, I got in touch with Vasiliy, the manager of the university campground whose house stood not far away from ours, but closer to the river. My forebodings were fulfilled. There was barely a sober day in Oleg's life after the New Year's night that he had spent with his daughter's family. I imagined the poor man afflicted since his return from the Afghan war and his poor dog, hungry and depressed, dwelling in the tiny house in this cosmic chill. During Oleg's binges, Mensch usually became detached. His shoulders hunched, his eyes guilty, he barely communicated with us as though Oleg's drinking was his fault.

I asked Vasiliy to update me when possible and thought about the best way to check on them. The hard frost and the road, plowed only occasionally, made travel difficult. Two weeks later, I received another message. Vasiliy found half-dead Oleg on the ice-covered river. He had gone fishing, drunk. If not for Mensch's barking, Oleg would have frozen.

At last, I reached Oleg on the phone and talked to him for half an hour. He sounded quite normal, though his voice was husky as if he was recovering from cold. He complained about Mensch's paw and asked me to buy vitamins for him, and I promised to take care of this. A few days later, Vasiliy called. He found Oleg dead in his bed. A collection of empty vodka bottles was a silent testimony of his lonely death. Oleg's daughter was going to take care of his house, and Vasiliy pledged to supervise the dog. Mensch lost everything at once—his master and his job.

During the spring months, I arranged a couple of trips to the cabin for a one-night stay and visited Mensch. In summer, we stayed in the cabin, Mensch with us. My heart clutched at the thought of the coming winter. The dog still got around but with great difficulty. Because of arthritis, he dragged his hind legs and couldn't use one of his forepaws. Instead, he bent it and walked on a joint that was worn to the bone he was constantly licking. We helped him onto the porch, and he howled for help when he needed to go down. Most of the time he simply dozed next to the porch, sun bathing with Boss who always followed him, waiting for him patiently. Boss seemed aware of Mensch's fading health.

The day of our return to the city approached, and my heart ached. Vasiliy promised to feed Mensch together with his other two dogs, but the old Husky barely ate anything.

A couple of weeks later, a phone call came from Vasiliy. Mensch refused to eat after we left, and he spent the past week under our porch without water. He asked me to put the dog asleep, "One shouldn't prolong Mensch's suffering."

With a heavy heart, I made the phone call to Maxim and reminded him of his patient, fifteen years old now, requesting his service. A long pause followed.

He cleared his throat. "Why don't you do it?"

"What do you mean?"

"I can fill a syringe with the drug, and you'll make the injection yourself. I'm very busy these days, and the trip would take up half a day."

Now was my turn to clear my throat. "You think I can?"

"Aren't you a nurse?"

"Yes."

"Then of course you can. Besides, you don't have any extra money. So, this way we'll help each other."

* * *

The next afternoon, I asked one of my friends to give me ride first to the vet and then to the cabin. As Vasiliy had reported, Mensch was under the porch, making no sound. When I entered the cabin and started preparing myself, he began whimpering.

I poured water into a bowl and crawled under the porch. Mensch lay on his side, his muzzle next to an empty water dish. He opened one of his eyes but showed no interest, so I wetted his lips with my fingers. He made no move, only wheezing. I put one of my hands under his cheek and caressed his faded coat with the other. I was bidding goodbye and asking Mensch for pardon—for not being always around, for not caring for him appropriately, for not loving him enough, not the way he loved all of us, me especially.

Who knows how long I would have stayed under the porch if not for Vasiliy. "Lena, are you done? The last bus is in one hour. You better hurry. And leave his body there. I'll take care of it."

I touched Mensch's disfigured face and opened the plastic bag containing the syringe. Taking a deep breath, I gathered my courage and slowly, as the vet instructed, injected the drug. Then I put my hand on his head and held it until I felt his heart stop beating and his breathing ceased. This was the second Mensch whose final breath I had caught and whom I escorted toward the threshold of life and death. I wrapped his body in a white sheet, looking at his frozen smile one last time. "We never cry," I whispered.

Nord Socialite

Fond of animals, I always wanted to have a dog. But why a dog? Maybe because dogs never lie about love. Or possibly because I was a celestial Dog myself. Indeed, Suzanne White says that Dog ladies need a tender pat, loving hugs, warm words of reassurance, and lots of playful romps in the woods to be happy.

So my puppy was a Shetland Collie, clumsy and fluffy like a teddy bear. For a few nights in a row, he desperately whimpered, searching for his lost mother in every corner. From the beginning, messages arrived from our friends and relatives: "Train the puppy! Don't let him sleep in the same bed with you. Puppies are fans of books, adventure stories in particular. They're also known for a great appetite for shoes and gloves."

We thoroughly studied the genealogical tree of our new family member and discovered he was the noblest feather among us, descending from German ancestors with blue blood for at least seven generations. It was clear his name had to be noble, too, so we called him Nord (German for "north").

Although we all enjoyed Nord's company, sharing the responsibilities for his care was a hard task, especially taking him out during cold Siberian winters. Another problem was keeping him clean. After six months, he transformed from a teddy bear to an elegant dandy with a white dickey on his chest and red-brown back. A luxurious tail reminiscent of an Arctic fox known for its exceptional beauty completed his outstanding apparel. His ensemble drastically disagreed with the outdoor conditions in our neighborhood—black snow piles throughout six winter months and puddled muddy streets during the other seasons. Because of this mud, our noble dog needed a full service treatment once back home. A partial service included just soaking his paws in a basin. But a better solution was a shower. Then, of course, the shaking, drying and combing.

As predicted, Nord invaded all the beds, sofas, and chairs, but unanimous resistance from our team finally forced him to accept our terms. While growing teeth, Nord indulged in slippers and occasionally victimized shoes, but books, easily accessible, never suffered damage. Nord would just stick his long, curious nose into a book as if looking for a title and then push it away. We were unable to figure out the reason behind his abstinence. Couldn't he read Russian? Or perhaps he had a little appreciation for our collection. Or possibly "No chewing!" was encoded in his genes.

Nord was an amazingly polite dog. He never poked around the kitchen, begging for food. In his teens, he developed a personal signal for requesting food. Sitting at the kitchen door, he would raise one of his front legs about six inches from the floor and hold it, pointing it down. No sound, no motion, merely a gesture. If one looked at him at that moment, he would divert his eyes as if ashamed. Nobody could resist such a silent and polite request.

All our efforts to train him as a home guard and to induce hostility toward intruders failed. Nord grew up a pacifist. This quality, of course, had certain advantages, especially during camping in summer. The university camping ground where we used to spend summers was full of kids of all ages. The ones who preferred to romp around with Nord, soliciting his touch, were preschoolers. Attacking Nord, they pushed him to the ground and rode on his back. Sometimes the dog was buried under half a dozen tiny bodies. Nord never complained. He knew they were human babies, though nobody taught him.

Once our Nord fell victim to his pacifistic nature and alien appearance—neither fox nor an ordinary dog. The Collie was introduced to Siberia only in the seventies and mostly in the cities, so cattle in the villages were unaware of this new breed. When we were camping, Nord was usually off leash, except during meals. To restrict his activities while we were dining in the communal shelter, I would tie him to a post next to our tent.

As soon as I shut the canteen's door on one memorable day and stepped out on the porch, I saw an unsolicited visitor maneuvering around our tent a couple of hundred yards away. Nord on a leash, confined in the space between two tents, desperately jerked hither and thither, trying to escape the sharp horns. Terrified, I screeched and activated all my resources, accelerating to the very limits as I ran to him. When I collapsed next to the dog, positioned to protect him, the cow reluctantly retreated. A sheepdog, fully equipped to fight against wolves, Nord declined to protect his own life. He neither attacked the cow nor even barked. Did he know the cow was not his enemy? That night, for the first time, I questioned the sanity of pacifism.

Camper Nord indulged in all our activities: running, swimming, boating, playing ball, and even hunting berries. There is a Russian kids' game called "A Little Dog." Two players throw a ball to each other, and the third tries to intercept it. Nord, of course, was the third player. Furiously swirling in the space between us, Nord whirled up, following the ball. When he caught it, he never gave it up right away. Instead, he made a ceremonial circle, wagging his red tail in triumph, his body twisting in a dance. If Nord danced too long, my son Pavel would attack him, and their entangled bodies rolled in the grass. After forfeiting the ball, Nord continued twirling in the tall grass or turned onto his back, exposing his belly submissively, his paws waving.

Wild strawberry patches were scattered around the camp ground, but mosquitoes guarded them safely, stealing the joy of short Siberian summers. Only in late August did they surrender to the laws of nature. By that time, the strawberry season was over. The desire to enhance scanty camping rations forced our occasional strikes into strawberries.

Decked out like beekeepers, we sneaked out of the camp together with the last drops of dew, heading to the birch woods. Nord customarily led our processions, his erected tail wagging, throwing out the golden sparkles of sunlight. Occasionally, he put his nose onto the ground and sniffed, digging holes. Kneeling on the forest floor, we combed the grass hunting for berries. When Pavel bumped onto the patch spattered with glittering berries, he gathered a handful and stretched his cupped palm to the dog. Nord put his nose into it, licked a few berries, and shuffled them into his mouth. Having savored for the first time what we were hunting for, he instantly turned into a gourmand and started begging.

"No, Sunshine! Don't give him more!" I ordered.

"But why? Poor Nord," my daughter Lena interfered.

"Let him find his own!" I said.

"But he doesn't have hands, Mom!" protested my son.

I turned back to the dog. He sat still, a single front paw raised above the ground, accompanied this time by the intense stare of his eyes. "Come on, Nord! Don't be so petty."

Nord turned away gloomy, but in a minute, he approached me.

"Come on!" I gave him a hug and gently pressed his nose to the berry. "Do you smell it? See how it is growing?" I picked the berry and put it in his mouth. He swallowed and gazed into my eyes with appreciation. "Search!" I commanded.

For a few seconds he reflected on his options; then, disregarding his nobility, Nord planted his forefeet on the ground and started crawling with us. His nose proved to be exquisite; immediately he found a hidden berry. Pulling out the delicacy together with a knot of grass, he enjoyed a strawberry salad, prepared by himself.

In winter, we harnessed Nord to pull sleds. When Pavel would lose the reins and fall into the snow, Nord would raise his tail victoriously and gallop away. He was a great runner, but not in deep snow. To extend his happy hours, our dog occasionally escaped and showed up late in the night, whimpering next to the entrance to the building, a prodigal son.

Spending days locked in the apartment, Nord longed for communication. He was a sociable dog, admiring the master in human. When we returned home, he used to give vent to his feelings of delight, exploding in bliss. The reception ritual included prancing, hugging, kissing, twirling around, wagging his tail, and boogie-woogie dancing, accompanied by his tenor yips. Nobody could surpass his expressions of love.

The hospitality of our dog was incurable. I remember March 8, the International Day of Woman. My colleagues agreed the party should be at my place. Because the men had to do all the cooking, they needed to leave the lab earlier. I gave them the apartment key together with the instructions for the kitchen.

"But how about the dog, Svetlana Alexandrovna? One of them consulted me."

"Just say hi!" I said.

"No joking?" He insisted.

I smiled back. "No joke."

The guys left early in the afternoon. About seven p.m. when I opened the door, the apartment was full. Nord, overwhelmed by affection for so many folks and by the festive atmosphere and the smell of delicious foods, shuffled delightfully, gesticulating with his fluffy tail. I myself received no traditional reception. Nord just shoved his head against my knee and turned back. As a real host, he was too busy entertaining the guests.

Only once, I recall him barking hostilely. It was when my daughter Lena introduced her boyfriend whom she married soon after. Nord squatted on his front legs, erected his tail, wrinkled his nose, and bared his fangs. He did not stop barking until the guy had left. Was he jealous, or trying to warn her? Perhaps both.

Nord fell victim to mating. His semen ducts ruptured, and the poor dog suffered something like peritonitis, a problem common to breed dogs as it turned out. The boyfriend of my daughter was in charge of his funeral.

Thirty years later, my memories of Nord are still as fresh as though it all had happened yesterday. His photos are preserved among others in our family album. His precious wool collected while combing and grooming him, I transformed into a beautiful jacket and mittens that soothed my joint pain. When strangers ask me what kind of wool is this, I reply, "Nordic."

Impressions

Without impressions there would be no Impressionists.

Until I found myself in the Arenberg Castle Park in Leuven, Belgium, I had no personal experience with birds. In Leuven, I spent two fruitful years working at the Catholic University, in the Metallurgy Department, situated next to the castle surrounded by the magnificent park. Luckily, I had to cross those grounds every day on my way to the department and back home, two twenty-minute trips. The castle was built by two families, in 1515 by William De Croy who was the chief-of-staff to Charles V, Holy Roman Emperor, and one hundred years later by the Arenberg family. The Duke of Arenberg donated the castle to the university. In 1783, from the front lawn of the Arenberg Park, a university professor launched history's first manned gas-filled balloon.

I was spellbound by the beauty of the park and the castle, a mixture of Gothic and Renaissance architecture. "Beauty will save the world," wrote Dostoevsky. I hope so, too, though people are becoming increasingly attached to the smart electronic devices and detached from each other and the environment, catching sight of the sky as reflections on their smart screens. Had I a smartphone in my hands, the beauty of the park and the mystery of the birds' lives would have easily escaped my attention and the learning opportunity would have been lost.

* * *

The elegant bird looked out of place among the numerous, clumsy ducks and obese, domestic geese—all inhabitants of a small pond at the center of the Arenberg Castle Park in Leuven, Belgium. Floating silently on the mirror of water, staring at its own reflection, it observed Earth and its inhabitants as if an alien from Planet Beauty. I thought of myself those days as a bird, too, migrating from one university to another, carrying my research and destiny. A bird, however, knows perfectly well its route and destination. I, however, did not.

This bird's plumage—an amalgam of beige and gray—iridescent in the sunlight, was delicate, smooth, and shiny. Like a pharaoh, it had chestnut makeup around its eyes and an inch-wide hoop of similar color around its neck.

The pastel beige of its back graduated into fox-red, its wings and tail, into onyx. I noticed my special bird residing in the magnificent park surrounding the castle in early spring. Each time I happened to be around, I greeted the mysterious and lonely creature with a bow. My sense of nostalgia, where did it come from? Whom was my solitary bird expecting? Was this pond a meeting point for lovers after a long separation, or perhaps a match-up site for escaping singlehood?

One day, when the sun was at its zenith, I settled on a stone bench a few feet away from the pond. My spectacular bird, momentarily frozen, seemed to be meditating on the smoothness and tranquility of the deep waters so contrasting the vanity on the ground. Three tiny rabbits, about a month old, were exploring the grass beneath an oak. Two brave ones devoured grass. The third kept close to the roots of the tree, his eyes wide-open, his little head always in motion, the body shivering. As soon as I repositioned myself on the bench, this little rabbit flashed into a hole under the tree. And I pondered which rabbits would survive—those who devoured grass disregarding danger, or the one always on guard with an empty stomach.

My bird felt comfortable in my presence, but I made sure not to take undue advantage of a blessed friendship; I watched and admired. Rain, the sun, and muddy water—bird's only accessories—kept its stylish apparel in a great shape. No French soaps, no facials. Only Mother Nature's care.

This idyllic state of tranquility was disturbed by two students. Farther away, where a span of swampy ground intersected the pond, these fellows were pouring buckets of cold and weedy water into a zinc trough, a contraption dated, perhaps, from the beginning of the 19th century. I was curious whether this performance was a bet or baptism of some kind. Neither of them looked like a priest to me. After filling the ancient trough, one, reminiscent of Don Quixote, pulled his clothes off and immersed himself in the water. The other fished a camera from his pocket and captured the scene on film. In five minutes, the silent performance was over, paraphernalia collected, and Don Quixote with his Pancho disappeared with dignity behind the castle.

A spring month of brief dates with the aristocratic bird on the pond passed quickly. Having exhausted my shoulders with computer work, abused my brain with non-stop production of scientific papers, I stretched my neglected body out on the stone bench, scanning the sky. Cloud formations and their transformations always attracted me. When fantastic cotton heads of various animals rearranged into familiar faces or equations, I enthusiastically read those messages on the blue board of eternity.

Sudden activity on the water interrupted my contemplation. Six tiny, weightless creatures, like black cotton balls, followed a water chicken. Did they really swim? No, they trotted on the surface of the water without disturbing it—a parade of a new generation full of innocent curiosity.

Weeks later, while walking to the windmill on the bridge near the castle wall, I passed alongside the grass thickets surrounding the pond. At first, I failed to realize what was happening there, but bird's agility struck me. The water chicken hopped out from the tall grass, grasped one of her chicks, and flashed back into the thickets. Having deposited the load there, she reappeared, furiously flapping her instantly grown wings at a black crow kidnapping her chicks. Who knows how many survived? No more parades after that incident.

The day I could not locate my favorite bird, I felt betrayed as I walked along the U-shaped pond. But as soon as I took a turn at the remote end—where a lush meadow stretched out to the walls of the grand ruins of the Duke's estate—I saw a scene that shed light on the behavior of my mysterious bird. This time, my fellow was surrounded by his family. His mate was slightly smaller but of similar stature and plumage, with only one difference; she had a brownish crown and no ring around her neck. The stately adults rose from the ground, nervously following my every move. Five fully-fledged juveniles, baseball size, carelessly stretched their treasured bodies guarded by the parents. The chicks seemed comfortable with this new mode of life after their lengthy incarceration inside the eggshell—a new generation of Egyptian geese, I recollected their family name I found recently on internet.

The three summer months were soon over. To finish a paper for an upcoming conference, I worked long hours in my attic office, always last to leave the building. On one occasion, dark came on instantly. The window pane hummed, attacked by the wind trying to break in. Dry swishing leaves blown down from the trees overhanging the roof performed a freakish dance, undecided which flight path to take—one leading straight to the ground, or the other into the darkness of the sinister sky—an eternal struggle of the opposites. Knocking persistently, the wind was throwing the first handfuls of rain drops at the unlocked window. The glass began weeping. At last, the windowpane blow-opened, surrendering to a gust, and the wild dance of the papers, caught up from my desk, flashed as if in Morse code: "Hurry, hurry! A storm watch is in effect!" I grabbed my umbrella and rushed out of the building.

Instead of taking my usual path along the edge of the pond, I raced along the stone-paved alley, straight to the castle whose arched gate, still open, might save me from the storm. The cypress hedge, between me and the pond, was rocking and falling; the gusts displayed the power of nature, bending the hedge capriciously.

Through one of the openings in this rocking hedge, my eyes caught a dramatic scene. In the middle of the meadow, on a ruined tall pedestal, a youngster from my bird family was testing the strength of its wings against the power of the storm. A gust of wind would lift the bird, its wings stretched four feet apart, and then subside, dropping the fledgling back onto the pedestal. Transfixed, I was afraid to scare the explorer and miss the moment of revelation—the bird's first flight!

While the young bird was struggling to fly, calculating pros and cons, the rest of the family members gathered in proximity, observing their fledgling's torments disapprovingly. The adults argued, exchanging angry sounds dampened by the toccata of the coming storm. Finally, the maverick took off. As soon as it was air born, it circled above its family, as if bidding farewell, and disappeared, carried by the wind. It was the first time I saw one of my birds fly. To tell the truth, I thought their wings had been clipped to keep them in the park.

For a few days, I saw only four youngsters on the meadow. The parents were obsessed with taking care of them. Whenever I tried to advance in their direction, they silently herded the teenagers away. The young birds obeyed the demands of the parents, clinging to them obediently, showing no interest in exploring the park full of other species. Theirs was disciplined kindergarten; I was puzzled how it happened that one of their brood matured much faster and managed to live alone, exposed to all the dangers of a modern city and predators, while the others enjoyed prolonged guardianship. I sympathized with the adventurer and explorer who challenged the great unknown.

One day, the family rested, spread on the slope near the pond, bathing in noon sunlight. I had almost passed their harmonious group when all of a sudden the silence was broken. The adults leaped up, yelling with raucous goose voices I'd had no chance to hear before. From nowhere, the adventurer re-appeared. In its impetuous flight, about thirty feet above the ground, the bird made an honorable circle, showing off aerobatics. The excitement of the parents was boundless. "Come, come, come!" they yelled in a duet, cocking their heads while following their child's flight. Surprisingly, the siblings showed no emotions. The prodigal son, however, soared up into the sky, made one more circle of honor, casting his impressive shadow, and disappeared behind the towers of the castle. How could I think these birds did not fly?

Occasionally I saw the young adventurer splashing on the smoothness of the water next to the family to spend a few minutes with them, yet detached. No exchange of news or particular tenderness did I notice during those brief visits home.

Interestingly, my bird family mixed neither with their own species whose numerous flocks I discovered later in the Leuven neighborhoods nor with other birds in the Arenberg Park. I believe this family were isolationists or outcasts. Also, unlike ducks and domestic geese, I never saw these birds begging humans for bread.

No bird feeding was allowed in the Arenberg Park, but every now and then, visitors broke this law to entertain their children. Domestic geese demanded crusts, hissing.

Advancing, they forced me to capitulate and leave my bench before my lunch break was over. Ducks, on the other hand, simply begged. Poorly balanced on the ground, they used to harvest bread and leave in peace. Once, I saw a procession of about fifty ducks following each other in a single file, pursuing a park officer. This queue reminded me of one I myself took part in, in the 1950's after the War, when I was a preschooler in Siberia, and bread was a great luxury.

On one occasion, I was lucky to observe the members of my bird family closer. A couple with children emerged from the arched gate of the castle. Approaching the pond, they were inspecting their bags and pockets for food. As soon as the visitors moved to the corner of the pond, near the gate to the castle, ducks hurried from all directions. When the children hurled the bread in the water, the ducks indulged, quarreling over every piece. The geese were farther away exploring the neighborhood, but they reacted fast. Disregarding their already full stomachs and heavy rear ends, those obese birds advanced with martial calls: Ga, Ga, Ga! In a few minutes, the goose squadron invaded, overtaking the ducks who simply fled the scene.

Before the feast, the outcast bird family rested in a remote corner of the pond, except for their patriarch who was in the middle—thirty feet away from his family and thirty feet away from the buffet. His mate and the youngsters were anxiously raising their gracious bodies and sinking back into the grass, their eyes locked on the feast corner, but none of them made a move towards it.

The patron himself was also overwhelmed. Gazing straight ahead, his wings flattened along his body, he marched along the waterfront, covering the distance to the site where his family rested, apparently trying to ignore the banquet. Haughtily erect, his wings tight to his body, he looked as though he wore a dress coat, reminding me of Napoleon depicted in his long coat, his hands behind him, marching thoughtfully before the decisive battle of Waterloo.

The nobility and independent character of the bird prevented him from joining the humiliating, free-for-all feast, and the family obeyed his mute order. The visitors seemed to be nearing the end of their bread supply, and this dramatic situation had to be resolved quickly. Hamlet's question "To be or not to be!" arose. Finally, Father turned to the water and entered it slowly, his head still raised high. At once, his family members followed his example, and in a matter of seconds, they covered the distance separating them from their patron. Their caravan approached the feeding party with perfect timing. Some bread crumbs were still floating on the surface of the water, and the Egyptian goose family harvested them without any fuss or fight, paying no attention to the domestic geese who, to my surprise, retreated.

* * *

The domestic geese usually took their long walks within the park, but occasionally they ventured through the open gate to the street, strolling there along sidewalks. Most often, the disciplined harem, guided by its Shah, fed peacefully on grass or promenaded alongside the pond. Forming an ideal straight line, the whole procession marched behind their leader, as he puffed himself with pride and greatness. Yet, "The Emperor was naked!"

Less adventuresome than the geese, the ducks always clustered in the proximity of the pond. At first sight, one might think they lived less remarkable lives obsessed with everyday routine, spending hours nibbling and stroking their wings, and feeding on the 'pond soup' rich in plankton. This impression turned out to be false.

Because of a strict dress code, there was no way for me to identify duck couples. While the males' plumage with the iridescent play of colors along the body and glossy green heads was rather extravagant, the females wore mainly humble brown-gray speckled coats. Based on the exquisite decoration of drakes' plumage, I concluded females picked up males. I also noticed drakes outnumbered females, harassing them constantly.

One of the ducks was an albino—reserved, distant, and gracious. I never saw her mix with the other ducks. Eventually, though, I noticed she acquired a partner, who followed her on the ground and in the water like a bodyguard.

Once on my way home, I passed a dormitory situated a hundred yards away from the creek that fed the pond densely populated by ducks. That evening, students had transformed the plaza in front of the building into a field kitchen. The smell of grilled meat took over other fragrances dominating that area of the park. Whiffs of smoke drifting across the creek stung my nose and eyes. The student party climaxed when the thunderous rock music rushed like an incessant tide through the open windows of the dormitory. While the students were deep into their intrigues intensified by an excess of sexual hormones and alcohol, here and there near the party site squabbles among the birds erupted.

I hurried along the path to avoid mixing my aura with the intoxicated crowd. Suddenly, from nowhere, a female duck appeared. In her effort to escape the male pursuing her, she dared to disperse the crowd, making a corridor, almost touching students' heads. Swishing the trembling air in her impetuous flight, she desperately called for help.

A bandit drake, whose furious onslaught threatened not just the duck's freedom of choice but her life, chased her viciously. A squadron of drakes followed them as often happens with teenagers looking for fun. What struck me most at the time was the orchestrated cooperation among the drakes.

One day, my initial observation about their cooperation was confirmed. That weekend, closer to the evening, the traffic of students through the park dwindled; the gray of early night began to prevail but had not yet condensed into gloom. Approaching a small bridge through the river circling the castle from the north, I spotted three ducks.

A bristled up albino, ducking towards the bridge, tried to escape a couple of drakes. Having noticed me, she maneuvered, turning back from the open grass to the thickets. This natural border slowed her down and failed her maneuver. Meanwhile, the pursuers reorganized, and she was trapped—confined from one side by the thickets and from the other by an ambushing drake-assistant. He pinned her tightly against the foliage to keep her in place. As soon as albino got trapped, the other drake mounted her, taking over. When his mission was accomplished, and the albino got her lesson, he and the drake-assistant withdrew from the stage with confidence.

The albino shook her shaggy, humiliated body and turned to the opposite direction where, about twenty feet away, I spotted her bodyguard. As if nailed to the ground, he was staring at her. Noticing her advancing toward him, he turned around and ducked away. This was the first time I saw the albino dragging behind her partner, and I could not help but wonder whether I had witnessed the duck's rape by one of the bachelors.

* * *

Despite the occasional quarrels in the flock of the domestic geese, the violent abuse of female ducks, and the infrequent visits of the black crow to the water chicken, bird life in the park seemed to proceed peacefully—no blood shed or dead bodies. Nevertheless, stray feathers scattered here and there silently pointed at those incidents I failed to witness, for my watch not twenty-four and seven.

The birds I observed every day crossing the park on my way to my department and back home were permanent dwellers of the park, the park I fell in love with and felt myself as its inseparable part. With changing seasons, it dramatically morphed—from light hues of green in the spring to purple in the fall, and to the black of the tree skeletons on the dazzling, turquois sky in the winter.

One morning when the scrubbed sky, washed in the dew, shone in ultramarine, I felt I could distinguish the flow of particles of light descending through the crowns of the trees, highlighting the intimate corners of the park now awakened from night dreams. Here and there a powerful beam illuminated shaggy branches of willows drooping into the creek. At these early hours, the wind had not yet breathed life into the trees, though just the day before, it seemed, it had played Chopin's lively etudes with those gracious willow's fingers now drowsily overlooking the creek. The city behind the monumental walls of the park was still asleep, though single cyclists and runners passed in a rush, reminding me of the inevitable vanity of the weekends, when Leuven residents of all four generations invaded the park.

Although the trees had failed to shake off their magnificent dreams, sparrows were already alert, bathing in the shallow puddles and grooming themselves. And in the middle of this peace and harmony, a drama was developing. Precisely in the center of the pond, about ninety feet away from a small stone bridge crossing the pool, a white swan, unseen before, rose over the mirror of the water. Majestically dressed in glossy, snow-white apparel, his head haughtily erect, he glided, surveying the neighborhood. The swan's posture and manners suggested a noble assessing a potential, new estate.

On the right side of the swan, slightly behind, a file of ducks followed. This elegant procession advanced in silence towards the stone bridge. Immediately, it became clear to me that the swan, a stranger, demonstrated his superior power, and the birds—the current residents—displayed their readiness to offer resistance. It seemed the swan paid no attention to the procession behind him, and the ducks showed no agitation either. Overtaking the swan, they turned to the right bank and one by one, keeping the same perfect order, exited the pond, climbing the slope—a perfectly orchestrated show of their own strength.

As soon as this group landed, another duck flotilla entered the water and began advancing towards the swan. Now, tension and electricity filled the air. The pressure exerted on the ducks by His Highness swan intensified so that the leader of the second group suddenly turned back as if surrendering. As soon as the leader abandoned the idea of resistance, the entire bird flotilla scattered, and the domination of the invader became an indisputable fact. His Highness silently ascended to the throne, taking over the current inhabitants of the pond.

After that, I always saw him alone. I thought his visit to the park might be just a brief stop on the way to an unknown destination. Instead, every morning, I spotted the bird in the same corner of the pond. Apparently, the invader decided to reside in this lovely estate, perhaps, until retirement.

Once, shortly after the swan's arrival, I found him promenading along the stone-paved path to the department building. I had to pass His Royalty but felt intimidated. He was the first swan I ever encountered closely, and I didn't know what to expect. Somehow, the cute little swans and the adorable white Princess Odette in the Tchaikovsky's ballet Swan Lake eclipsed the character of the Black Swan, leaving me less fearful. At last, I passed His Royalty and hurried away promptly. Ten yards later, I drew a deep breath, relieved.

Here and there, I saw the swan stretching his long neck along the bank slope, feasted on the grass and grunted like a boar. A boar! I could not imagine how such majestic bird could emit a sound like this. Gradually the image of magical, little swans from Swan Lake faded in my head to be replaced by a new character. Bit by bit, this character took over not only the pond but also all neighboring grounds. It seemed he could be everywhere simultaneously. His walking tours constantly expanded until the entire pond with all adjacent alleys were under the control of the occupant. Pedestrians, instead of enjoying their walks, hastily escaped those narrow passages framed by cypress hedges when His Highness was in the view.

One day closer to the fall, I invited a colleague for a walk, although the weather had turned drizzly. Mist caressed my face while we spoke softly. Noticing the swan at a distance, we stopped at the bank, reflecting upon the lonely presence of the bird wrapped in the whitish mist.

Much to my surprise, as soon as the swan became aware of us, he began steering in our direction. Having landed at the bank, he rushed up along the slope, his wings wide spread. Standing on the wet stone-paved path about ten feet from the waterfront, I had no clue of his intentions.

Instinctively I pointed my umbrella at the bird, trying to keep him away, but this trick was no help. I panicked and backed up, and lost my balance. As I hit the ground, I fortunately curled and avoided a collision with a short pole in the middle of the path, placed there to deter cars from entering.

The astonished bird halted while my colleague, a mathematician, silently observed the whole scene, his face slack-jawed with amazement. Instead of reaching out a hand to help me, he muttered, "What an excellent fall that was! You curled up into a perfect cochleoid of Eratosthenes." He rounded his hands to show the arch my body instinctively acquired. Picking myself up from the ground and patting my skinned hand, I cursed everybody: the swan, myself, my colleague, and Eratosthenes—whoever he could be.

A few days later, when the weather mellowed, I was back at the meadow on a stone bench next to the pond. Settled down with my humble belongings, a book and a bottle of water, I stretched out on the bench enjoying the warmth of the midday sun and the loving energy of the earth. Alas, my relaxation was short-lived: from nowhere, my tyrant appeared, heading directly towards my bench. Not brave enough to claim my first right to this part of the pond and the bench in particular, I grasped my belongings and hastily retreated.

The next day during lunch hour, I was crossing the meadow, chatting with a graduate student. The swan was far away in the corner of the park. As soon as we came into his view, he decisively changed his route, advancing in our direction. Although I knew the swan was after me, my companion, who had heard about my case and Eratosthenes, was unwilling to be the swan's next victim. Hastily, we backed up, taking a different route. Shortly we emerged from behind a huge tree in the center of the meadow face-to-face with this mean creature who had outsmarted us and cut us off. Thus, the magnificent park became an exclusive property of the despot.

Soon, however, unexpected news arrived: the swan had taken over a plaza in front of the castle and blocked the noon car traffic from both directions, assuming the new role of traffic patrol officer. This incident was the last straw; the swan was arrested by the park's police and banished from the park. A sigh of relief rumbled through its domains. The bird, uncompromising, willing to share nothing, lost everything as it often happens to us, humans. Life in the park stabilized once more, and again I felt myself an essential part of it, expecting no other invaders.

* * *

The pond and the meadows in the park, especially a large front lawn of the chateau, happened to be rest stations for migrating Canada geese. Stopping there briefly, the birds found needed rest during long journeys. Spread over the lawn, still wet with the morning dew, they combed the ground foot by foot like minesweepers. No food escaped those troopers—monumental, fit, and sturdy enough to undertake exhausting flights. In the sky, they rely only on the strength of their wings and the brotherhood of the flock. Domesticated geese lose these features. Acquiring one privilege, we humans likewise often lose an ability in its place.

These were Canada geese who taught me an unforgettable lesson about the strength of brotherhood. During a short student break, a week before my departure from Leuven for good, I had the park at my disposal. A small raft, half-immersed in the water, provided me a place to peacefully contemplate the deep sky. A young pine, just a few feet away from the waterfront, offered comforting shade.

A subtle breeze combing the water turned the mirror-smooth pond into a 3D-wave structure. Tiny ripples followed each other in perfect order and timing. It was about six, and the sun was beginning to set. Before bidding a final goodbye, it played with the ripples which readily gathered the sun's energy and instantly reflected it, sparkling as though laughing. I noticed as reflected sunlight hit the branches, then hurried from branch tips to the trunk of the pine, twinkling. It made a spellbinding animated picture I had never seen before.

Absorbed by the magic of the play between wind, light, and water with the charming pine, I failed to notice a huge flock of geese in the sky. The tip of the flock was a perfect V, which I always believed stood for victory. One of the ends of the long pattern was constantly reconstructing itself. I instantly understood there was a painful drama going on about to climax. One of the geese was falling behind, and two others alternated between the flock and the feeble fellow, providing company to the unfortunate bird.

All at once, I was overwhelmed by the intensity of their drama. Empathizing with the bird striving against the increasing distance to the flock and feeling the anxiety and concern of the two other fellow-birds, I leaped up. Having straightened myself like an antenna, I sent my prayers upward to the pilgrims.

Eventually, after multiple trips, one of the birds sympathizing with the feeble goose re-joined the flock, but the other stayed behind. Gradually, the sky gap between them lengthened, and the flock disappeared beyond the horizon, leaving the pair behind them.

For a long time after the scene I witnessed, I continued to contemplate the sky, musing whether in the behavior of the geese I observed an expression of compassion and altruism, the highest emotions among humans. And I felt the park with its inhabitants and passersby somehow opened to me, allowing me to understand the language of its dwellers and their lives. I knelt on the raft and said good bye to the park, to the birds, and to the university after spending two fruitful years there.

Japanese Delights

This restaurant is so small the four of us can barely squeeze together in front of the counter, facing a sushi chef who seems delighted to have early visitors. He bows reverently to each of my colleagues as he hands out menus. A strong sea weed aroma emanates from the wall where gifts of the sea are stored on ice in baskets, next to live fish in a large aquarium.

Wow! The menu, with more than thirty sushi varieties, is impressive, but I am not a sushi lover. Salted-overnight raw salmon agrees with me pretty well, but completely raw fish? No. So I order conservatively: seaweed salad with small pieces of salmon and *ikura* (caviar) sushi.

My companions are locked in a gourmand discussion of sushi, and I can't help them. Let me choose a beverage. Aha! Here they are: "Cola, Ginger Ale, Milk, Flesh Juice!" Well, Flesh Juice sounds challenging. I'd better skip it.

There are also "Alcools [sic]: Beer, Cocktail, and Sake." Sake. The Japanese use it for all occasions—to deal with cold or heat, to get high or low, or to fill the gas tank. Hundreds of wooden sake barrels next to a shrine, we saw earlier this morning— silent testimony to my observations. The chef, wearing a Mona Lisa smile, pours sake from a ceramic container into small ceramic cups. The clear drink made from a sweet rice scalds my tongue. Too strong for my taste. My body instantly warms, globally.

Oh, Jesus! Will they ever finish this sushi-sushi-sushi discussion? Let me wash my hands.

A sign we ignored upon entering the restaurant reads: "For Restrooms, go back toward your behind." Fine! Following the instructions precisely, I do find the place and barely fit in. Accomplishing my task, I turn and read another sign on the door: "You lady will push this button before leaving." In another country, I would be insulted or feel freedom-of-choice-deprived, but instead, I obey this categorical tone to avoid any international conflicts. Who knows? They are wired differently here in the Land of the Rising Sun, and I am not ready for hara-kiri yet.

Returning to the counter, I see my sushi has been served, and there is a new customer, a Japanese man, sitting on the far left side of the aisle. Listening to my companions and occasionally throwing a word into the discussion, I close my eyes and swallow a generously spiced sushi, anticipating turmoil in my stomach. In the meantime, the chef, armed with a dip net, catches a swimmer from the aquarium and puts it on the operating table about four feet from me. Since I sit exactly across the aquarium, also about four feet away, a strange Bermuda Triangle forms.

To my amazement, the rest of the fish in the aquarium stop dancing around and park in the corner of the tank closest to the chef. The live fish on the cutting board leaps, fighting for oxygen, trying to escape its destiny. All in vain. A sharp knife, in a few precise movements, scrapes away its flesh from both sides, leaving only a thin transparent layer next to the spine. The head and tail remain intact after this mutilation.

Consumed with empathy for the living creature, I ask, "What kind of fish is this?"

"Sushi," the chef replies, his face smooth and round as gravel.

"Is this the name of the fish?" I persist, trying to squeeze bits of information about this unfortunate creature whose death throes I just witnessed.

"Yes, yes," he nods with an invariable bow.

Yet I am not certain whether this is a sushi fish or fish used to make sushi. He is uniformly dark gray, about eight inches long, and has a tail fin strongly curved in the middle and sharply tipped; the head perfectly matches the V-shape opening of the fin. The mutilation is over. The chef takes a sharp bamboo stick, skewers it through the fish along the spine, stands it vertically on the plate, and places this exhibit in front of the Japanese man.

In total shock, I stare. The fish or, better said, what is left of the fish—its skeleton and nervous system—is still in agony. The convulsions spread from head to tail.

I gaze at the Japanese man who devours sushi rolls, ignoring the writhing animal on the plate in front of him. I cannot bear it and turn away towards the aquarium. The chef steps aside, allowing me an unobstructed view of the aquarium and the counter.

"Look here!" I call to my companions, absorbed in their meals. I gesture, connecting the observant, motionless fishes in the aquarium with the tortured fellow. "Look at the other fishes! See, they are all frozen in this corner, across from the spot where their mutilated fellow is displayed."

"Yes, right," one of my companions agrees, "they are staring."

"Exactly!" I exclaim.

"What is going on here?" Another one questions.

"Don't you see? It's like a crowd watching an execution. Imagine the fishes are spectators and the plate on display is a scaffold, and you will get the right picture."

Forgetting their meals, everyone watches the drama unfolding in the aquarium and on the counter, their faces perplexed. The only visitor with no gleam of animation in his gray face is the Japanese customer.

To avoid witnessing the finale, I pay my bill and tell my companions I will wait outside. Turning to the exit, I face another masterpiece of contemporary *Engrish*: "Please keep chair on position, keep table cleaned after dying. Thank you for corporation."

"*Arigato Gozaimas*," shouts the chef, bowing and smiling broadly at me for the first time as if mocking me.

Tsukuba, 2006

Open Letter from a Dog

Dear Bipeds,

Most of you, outraged by our existence, simply have no pets. Occasionally, you wouldn't mind having one, but not a dog. Why? FYI, dogs have a very high IQ, just below humans and other apes. But never mind. We, dogs, deal with horses, cows, and sheep. Fulfilling our duties, we ease the burdens of humans in their domestic endeavors and foreign affairs. Not only do we hunt with you to put food on your table, but we also guard your hearth, ready to sacrifice our lives at the very first call.

Despite all of this, you place us below cattle. Let's face it, cows don't work for the police. They don't detect bombs and drugs, defending the safety and security of the nation, risking their lives all the while. Unlike us dogs, cows aren't even trained to predict earthquakes or tsunami, or sniff out cadavers. Incidentally, although dogs are the real guardians of peace, as opposed to some other recipients, a dog has never been awarded the Nobel Prize.

What about those dogs lending their eyes to the blind? Those dogs harnessed to sleds which no cattle or horse could pull? And what about our siblings sacrificed for the advancement of science, your health, your longevity? And those dogs serving in elderly homes and psychiatric hospitals, drawing your brothers and sisters out of their isolation and depression? And what about dogs smelling cancers and impending epileptic fits? Don't you have an appreciation for those professionals? And how about those Russian stray dogs who were the first to orbit the Earth?

But let's go straight to your pretensions. You, fellows, often wonder why dogs are always around. Whoops! You're looking for answers. Those more advanced among you may even say that dogs give love humans can't. Bingo! They've got it right! Love isn't easy because humans love conditionally, while a dog's love is for the sake of love itself.

Curiously enough, we dogs comprehend you regardless of your language. Unerringly, we discern between good and evil without even going to church. As unlikely as it may seem, two hundred words is quite enough to understand you. There are Einsteins among us, too, who can easily master up to nine hundred words, which some of you can barely handle.

Some of you, intellectuals, notice the Big Books do not explicitly say how humans should treat other species; neither the Bible, nor the Constitution, nor the Declaration of Independence. So we are sold and purchased like inanimate possessions. Shouldn't you make at least an amendment to the Constitution? Perhaps something like: "The citizens shall not harm dogs and cats, nor other innocent animals, and shall treat them with the respect they are due." Aren't we entitled to a few fundamental moral and legal rights? And how about the right to vote? Woof? It's never too late to make these adjustments.

Those in politics always point to the association between American presidents and dogs. Does one really need a dog to become an American president? Barak was elected without a dog though he promptly acquired one, then another. Whatever the roots of this trend, those weapons of mass-destruction detected by George W. Bush would have been easily located, had they existed to begin with, if only he had Barney's sensitive nose. Do you follow me? Woof? Woof?

In the final analysis, dearest citizens of the most advanced country in the world, you say that you are dreaming big and stronger than ever before. But I'll tell you this: shamelessly you call the nation backward, not towards transformation and the future but towards a restoration of yesterday's America. As a dog, I ask you: how low must America descend to be restored? Perhaps abolish equal rights, or reinstate slavery? Or even better— to undomesticate us dogs? Woof? Woof? Woof? What the woof's going on?

And how about the state of economy? Here and there, we overhear complains about dog's spending. Nonsense! Guess what, too many Americans are seriously in debt! We dogs don't ask for anything. Don't blame us. Just think! Do we use bank accounts? Credit cards? Take out loans? I tell you, dogs are poor businessmen. We are barkers, not bankers. We don't run insurance companies or stock markets. If we partake in the judicial system, it is at a very low level. Please, direct concerns with your economy to an appropriate address. A dog wouldn't give a flea's behind for it.

After all is said, I don't buy it when those of you who hate us most claim to have animal magnetism. No! Dogs do not make such mistakes. If we pee on you, there is a reason, not magnetism. Lifting a hind leg against the nearest upright object and letting urine escape is a peaceful ceremony established by dogs to mark the areas of their interest, preemptively. Check Wikipedia. Marking you, we merely acknowledge you're a new bar-coded vertical protrusion to us. Another reason? To convert you, to integrate you, to humanize you, say I, the Dog.

Acknowledgments

I could not have written this story collection without the help of our cats: Cezanne, Matisse, and The Thing who not only opened their lives to us but became our true companions, overcoming their feline narcissism; without my daughter, Lena, who shared with me her odyssey with her family and her dogs and cats depicted in *The Way Our Animals Love Us*; without my niece Irina who told me the story of love and devotion of a little parrot, Prosha. A cycle of stories about birds combined under the title *Impressions* represents my first steps in writing. It was the beauty of the Arenberg Castle Park in Leuven, Belgium that cast a spell on me, inspiring daydreams that eventually materialized on the paper. I also have to thank *Engrish.com* for complementing my Japanese experience. I am grateful to my husband, Athan Petridis, for his support and encouragement, and for accepting my non-physics face, which revealed itself when I returned to the US. I am thankful to the writers of the WDM Library Group who at first could only hear a musical accent in my reading but eventually began decoding the meaning, encouraging my writing. I am also obliged to my first and faithful editor, Zachary Harper, who was always able to decipher my encrypted writing; to Marianne Fons for her thoughtful editing, to Veva Larson for her final touch, and to my first Kindle reader, Darryl Eschete, who volunteered to groom the manuscript.

About the Author

Svetlana Alexander is the pen name of Svetlana Shabalovskaya. Born in Siberia and educated at Tomsk State University in Physics (Ph.D. and D.Sc.), she resided in the US in 1994. Pursuing her research on metallic biomaterials, she also worked in Belgium, Germany, and Italy. For her career longevity and unwavering excellence in her research field, she is a recipient of *Albert Nelson Marquis Lifetime Achievement Award*. The collection of short stories, *A Is for Animals*, is her debut in a new field she is actively exploring. Her first novel, *Crimes of Hearts* or *A Glimpse behind the Iron Curtain*, is going to be published soon after. She is living with her husband in West Des Moines, Iowa, and she has two adult children.

97939677R00064

Made in the USA
San Bernardino, CA
27 November 2018